500 GAMES

(Originally published under the title
The Whitbread Book of 500 Party Games)

Compiled by PETER L. CAVE

Illustrations by KATHLEEN WHAPHAM

Publishers · GROSSET & DUNLAP · New York

A Note About This Book

PARTY GAMES can keep a party going, start a party, act as pleasant time fillers or as ways of getting to know people. Over the years it has become traditional for some games to be played by very small children only and others by adults only, yet surprisingly enough adults can have a lot of fun playing games designed for small children, and often the reverse is also true.

For that reason we have not carefully sub-divided games saying they are *only* available for one age group. The early pages suggest a number of guidelines but we think that if you flip through the book you will be given a lot of ideas for a lot of games that will be a lot of fun for you, however old or however young you are. Remember the ages are merely a guide.

Safety. Remember, too, that small children playing lively games can give themselves nasty bruises on furniture that would not harm an adult. With this in mind, try to pick the right play area for each game according to the age and number of the players.

Grosset & Dunlap, Inc.

1988 Printing

ISBN: 0-448-02159-5

© Wolfe Publishing Limited, 1970.
Originally published under the title
The Whitbread Book of 500 Party Games.

Printed in the United States of America.

To Help You Choose

To help you to find just the right games for your particular party, we have given each game a number, and grouped the numbers into sections for easy reference. Minimum ages have been suggested in the two main sections to give some guidance on the suitability of the games. Look up the section, look up the number — and have a really great party.

SPECIALLY GOOD ICEBREAKERS

20, 77, 86, 90, 119, 124, 125, 129, 145, 206, 216, 276, 281, 282, 295, 326, 327, 328, 381, 414, 415, 425, 482, 486, 492, 493

INDOOR GAMES
For any age over 5 or 6

7, 10, 12, 15, 16, 17, 18, 23, 26, 31, 36, 38, 43, 50, 51, 55, 65, 66, 67, 70, 81, 83, 95, 96, 104, 108, 121, 131, 147, 155, 158, 162, 169, 170, 171, 173, 178, 180, 182, 183, 190, 191, 192, 193, 197, 198, 201, 204, 211, 227, 233, 234, 236, 237, 242, 244, 245, 255, 257, 262, 269, 276, 286, 293, 295, 297, 298, 301, 303, 304, 308, 349, 383, 403, 404, 410, 416, 417, 457, 472, 499, 500

For any age over 6 or 7

5, 6, 8, 11, 13, 20, 32, 33, 35, 37, 40, 44, 46, 78, 92, 94, 100, 101, 103, 105, 106, 115, 119, 126, 136, 160, 166, 174, 175, 176, 212, 221, 231, 254, 261, 263, 264, 265, 268, 278, 280, 289, 290, 291, 294, 305, 306, 322, 341, 345, 347, 353, 366, 369, 377, 379, 380, 381, 389, 394, 396, 399, 411, 415, 440, 451, 475, 478, 490, 494

For any age over 7 or 8

2, 3, 14, 30, 48, 99, 111, 112, 120, 132, 135, 142, 157, 164, 165, 167, 179, 205, 207, 222, 248, 258, 266, 267, 287, 302, 318, 320, 323, 330, 354, 374, 385, 392, 393, 395, 398, 400, 405, 409, 412, 413, 419, 428, 452, 453, 456, 497

For any age over 8 or 9

28, 53, 77, 79, 87, 91, 109, 130, 153, 156, 186, 216, 217, 223, 224, 247, 277, 282, 284, 285, 321, 327, 328, 343, 344, 361, 362, 363, 364, 367, 368, 371, 372, 375, 386, 387, 388, 448, 473, 498

For any age over 9 or 10

22, 49, 72, 74, 75, 85, 107, 125, 128, 200, 283, 324, 325, 335, 346,

351, 356, 357, 358, 359, 360, 370, 382, 384, 397, 418, 423, 427, 462, 474, 479, 491, 496

From 10 upwards/For any age
1, 24, 47, 73, 88, 90, 114, 116, 117, 118, 122, 123, 124, 133, 134, 139, 140, 141, 143, 145, 146, 161, 172, 187, 203, 206, 252, 281, 299, 300, 319, 329, 331, 332, 333, 334, 350, 365, 373, 422, 424, 425, 432, 442, 445, 446, 447, 454, 460

OUTDOOR GAMES
For any age over 5 or 6
31, 45, 50, 65, 67, 104, 121, 131, 137, 155, 163, 168, 178, 181, 183, 194, 196, 197, 198, 213, 214, 215, 234, 235, 236, 237, 238, 239, 242, 245, 246, 256, 301, 303, 304, 307, 308, 403, 426, 449, 457

For any age over 6 or 7
20, 25, 29, 42, 82, 102, 103, 113, 136, 160, 220, 278, 305, 366, 377, 379, 381, 389, 420, 450

For any age over 7 or 8
54, 110, 111, 135, 151, 188, 202, 222, 232, 240, 243, 323, 339, 352, 385, 392, 409, 419, 421, 452, 455, 456, 458

For any age over 8 or 9
19, 218, 219, 260, 275, 292, 336, 340, 388, 448

For any age over 9 or 10
107, 128, 152, 338, 397, 427, 429

From 10 upwards/For any age
4, 139, 152, 161, 203, 218, 219, 251, 260, 292, 336, 338, 340, 365

Games more suitable for boys only
54, 56, 128, 152, 161, 202, 203, 232, 237

GAMES FOR THE UNDER-FIVES
21, 27, 34, 41, 56, 57, 58, 59, 60, 61, 62, 63, 64, 68, 69, 71, 80, 93, 97, 98, 138, 144, 148, 149, 150, 159, 177, 184, 185, 189, 195, 208, 209, 210, 241, 249, 250, 253, 270, 271, 272, 273, 274, 309, 310, 311, 312, 313, 314, 315, 316, 317, 337, 433

GAMES FOR TEENAGERS

9, 39, 52, 76, 84, 86, 89, 127, 199, 225, 226, 228, 251, 259, 279, 348, 355, 376, 378, 390, 408, 414, 441, 461, 476, 480, 488, 492, 493, 495

GAMES FOR ADULTS

9, 39, 52, 76, 84, 86, 127, 129, 154, 199, 228, 229, 230, 279, 288, 296, 326, 342, 348, 355, 376, 378, 390, 391, 401, 402, 408, 414, 430, 431, 434, 435, 436, 437, 438, 439, 443, 461, 464, 476, 477, 480, 481, 482, 483, 484, 485, 486, 487, 488, 489, 495

GAMES NEEDING NO EQUIPMENT

12, 19, 20, 30, 39, 47, 48, 49, 52, 54, 56, 57, 58, 59, 60, 61, 63, 67, 71, 83, 87, 88, 89, 90, 93, 94, 95, 96, 97, 106, 107, 111, 124, 131, 135, 137, 142, 143, 145, 146, 148, 149, 150, 151, 152, 156, 157, 161, 163, 167, 171, 173, 175, 177, 183, 185, 188, 189, 190, 195, 197, 198, 199, 202, 205, 206, 207, 214, 215, 222, 223, 225, 226, 227, 232, 234, 235, 237, 238, 239, 243, 244, 247, 252, 253, 256, 257, 265, 267, 269, 270, 271, 273, 274, 277, 282, 288, 296, 301, 303, 304, 305, 307, 310, 311, 312, 313, 314, 315, 316, 318, 337, 345, 346, 348, 349, 350, 351, 353, 355, 373, 377, 380, 381, 382, 384, 385, 389, 397, 408, 409, 412, 413, 414, 416, 422, 423, 424, 425, 426, 427, 452, 454, 455, 457, 462, 465, 466, 470, 471, 488

TEAM GAMES

1, 2, 5, 6, 10, 14, 15, 35, 38, 40, 41, 42, 47, 57, 67, 70, 85, 92, 93, 96, 102, 103, 107, 110, 112, 113, 114, 119, 120, 121, 127, 128, 129, 132, 140, 152, 158, 169, 172, 173, 180, 184, 187, 196, 200, 202, 205, 209, 212, 214, 218, 219, 220, 223, 237, 240, 243, 251, 254, 265, 266, 275, 276, 284, 285, 289, 290, 291, 292, 294, 295, 323, 330, 341, 347, 350, 355, 365, 370, 371, 372, 376, 377, 378, 379, 385, 388, 389, 390, 391, 392, 393, 394, 396, 397, 398, 400, 413, 418, 426, 427, 430, 431, 433, 451, 456, 458, 489, 496, 497, 500

BOISTEROUS GAMES

4, 5, 6, 19, 27, 54, 65, 82, 100, 110, 128, 131, 135, 137, 140, 161, 162, 168, 202, 203, 213, 214, 215, 218, 232, 235, 236, 238, 239, 256, 257, 292, 294, 303, 304, 305, 307, 308, 377, 386, 389, 426, 451, 452

'PARTNER' GAMES
16, 19, 48, 49, 54, 55, 56, 77, 86, 101, 124, 151, 161, 197, 203, 236, 239, 241, 249, 263, 267, 269, 271, 278, 281, 301, 303, 304, 305, 322, 327, 328, 351, 380, 395, 401, 402, 414, 415, 425, 452, 457, 461, 472, 473, 474, 488, 493

MUSICAL GAMES
18, 23, 26, 27, 55, 80, 138, 144, 159, 210, 241, 245, 250, 279, 281, 283, 293, 295, 297, 298, 410, 453, 461, 480, 492, 493

SINGING OR DANCING GAMES
20, 57, 58, 59, 60, 61, 62, 63, 73, 93, 97, 98, 148, 225, 226, 270, 272, 282, 310, 311, 312, 313, 314, 341, 417, 461, 492, 493

PENCIL AND PAPER GAMES
13, 53, 72, 99, 103, 116, 117, 118, 123, 154, 155, 164, 165, 166, 174, 179, 182, 299, 300, 319, 322, 324, 325, 326, 329, 331, 333, 334, 335, 344, 391, 405, 468, 472, 473, 474, 475, 479, 483, 491

WORD GAMES AND QUIZZES
33, 39, 40, 47, 48, 49, 52, 53, 74, 75, 76, 79, 85, 87, 88, 89, 90, 91, 94, 99, 103, 106, 111, 123, 125, 133, 141, 142, 143, 145, 146, 153, 156, 157, 164, 165, 167, 172, 183, 199, 206, 207, 222, 223, 227, 247, 248, 252, 277, 300, 318, 329, 330, 331, 332, 333, 334, 342, 344, 373, 382, 384, 391, 397, 408, 412, 413, 424, 428, 448, 462

PARTY TRICKS AND PUZZLES
406, 407, 444, 459, 463, 464, 465, 466, 467, 468, 469, 470, 471

CARD GAMES
2, 33, 40, 212, 276, 320, 356, 357, 358, 359, 360, 440, 441, 442, 443, 445, 446, 447, 460

DARTS GAMES
132, 228, 229, 230, 430, 431, 434, 435, 436, 437, 438, 439

1 AD GUESSING

Any age over 12 or 13 – Teams of equal numbers – Indoors – Equipment: 36 well-known advertisements.

Place around the room thirty-six advertisements cut out from various papers and magazines with the product name removed. Divide the players into teams and stand them all together in the centre of the room. The host then calls out the name of a product, and it is up to the members of each team to find the corresponding advertisement. The winning team will be the one which has collected most advertisements. A similar competition is for the referee to call out a clue; and the competitor should automatically look for the appropriate advertisement . . . Again, the winning team is the one with the most advertisements collected.

2 ACES HIGH

Any age over 7 or 8 – Teams of equal number – Indoors – Equipment: 12 Aces from 3 packs of cards, plus 12 other cards.

Hide twelve aces from three packs of playing cards around the room, together with twelve other cards. Divide the players into two or more teams. The referee then calls out a clue – for example, if a card is hidden under a clock, he might say: 'What is the time?'. It is then up to the competitors to find the card. The team with the most aces is declared the winner. N.B. It's hard luck if your team guesses the twelve clues correctly, and picks up twelve playing cards that are not aces . . . but it's all in the game.

3 RICE PICKING

Any age over 7 or 8 – Any number – Indoors – Equipment: for each player 12 grains of rice on a plate and 2 unsharpened pencils.

Using only the pencils, the players must lift the grains of rice out of the plates. The first one to clear his plate wins.

4 JUMPING JACKS

For children of 10 or over — Any number — Outdoors — Equipment: children's hats plus (possibly) some books.

This is a game for strong girls and boys. One volunteer makes a back for leapfrog, placing his feet wide apart, his hands on his knees, and the competitors take turns springing over, straddle-legged, each placing a hat on the back as they go. As the pile of hats grows higher and the jumping more difficult, you will find people knocking over the pile. When this happens, they drop out. If there is more than one competitor left when all the hats have been placed, then balance two or three books on top of the hats . . . You will soon find the winner.

5 BAG BLOW RELAY

Any age over 6 or 7 — Any even number — Indoors — Equipment: a paper bag for each child.

Set out two equal rows of chairs with a paper bag on each. At the word 'GO', the first member of each team runs once round his row of chairs, goes to the first chair in his row, blows up the bag and bursts it. When it has burst, the second team member takes off — and so on. The first team to burst all its bags is the winner.

6 BALLOON RELAY

Any age over 6 or 7 — Any even number — Indoors — Equipment· a blown-up balloon on each chair.

A similar game to Bag Blow Relay, but one that can at times leave a sting in the bottom. Place a blown-up balloon on each of two rows of chairs and form up two teams, each standing behind a chair. At the word 'GO' Number One in the team dashes around his row of chairs, and when he returns to his original chair he sits down heavily on the balloon. He must burst it before Number Two in the team continues along the same lines. The winning team will be fully seated with a burst balloon under each one.

7 BLIND MAN'S BUFF

Any age from 5 or 6 — Any number — Indoors — Equipment: a blind-fold.

Take it in turn to blindfold one member of the party and let him or her loose to roam around the room. The blindfolded player must place his or her hands on someone and guess who he has caught. If successful, then it is the turn of the person caught to be blindfolded.

8 PAPER PUZZLE

Any age over 6 or 7 — Any number — Indoors — Equipment: one newspaper for each player.

Sit your guests closely together in a circle. Give each child a well-mixed-up newspaper and be prepared for a ripping time. On the word 'GO' the contestants must reassemble the pages of the paper in the correct order. The tighter you sit the players, the more difficult it becomes.

9 SLOSHY

Teenagers or adults — Any number — Indoors — Equipment: a cup, an ice cube and a pair of drinking straws for each player, some warm water and a plate for the ice.

A lump of ice is dropped into a cup of warm water. This has to be retrieved, using only the drinking straws as chopsticks, before it melts. The person who fishes out the biggest lump is the winner. Sticks made out of tightly-rolled cardboard may be used instead of drinking straws.

10 BALL BOWLING

Any age from 5 or 6 — Teams of 4, 5 or 6 people — Indoors — Equipment: 12 match boxes or cigarette packets, and a tennis ball for each team.

Set out in a triangular pattern twelve matchboxes or empty cigarette packets and form teams of four, five or six people. Give each team a tennis ball to bowl along the floor at the packets. Each player is allowed two turns, and the number of packets knocked down will be added to the team score.

11 CATCH THE CANE

Any age from 6 or 7 — Any number — Indoors — Equipment: a small cane.

Players 'disguised' as towns sit in a circle. The odd man out stands in the centre of the circle holding a small cane. He then calls out a name of a town, throws the cane in the air, and the person representing that town must catch the cane before it hits the floor. If the competitor fails to catch the cane in time he has to drop out of the game. If he is successful, he takes over as odd man out in the centre of the circle.

12 DO THIS/DO THAT

Any age from 5 or 6 – Any number – Indoors – Equipment: none.

One player is responsible for carrying out actions prefaced by 'DO THIS' or 'DO THAT'. If he says 'DO THIS' then the players do it. If he says 'DO THAT' then they don't do a thing. Anyone who doesn't do this when he should or does do that when he shouldn't is 'out'. The last person still doing this and refusing to do that wins. Example: The caller could stand on one leg, prefacing his action by saying 'DO THIS' or 'DO THAT'.

13 DRAW THE LINE

Any age over 6 or 7 – Any number – Indoors – Equipment: a column of newsprint and a pencil for each player.

Sit the players round a table (or provide them with something to rest on) and give them all columns of newsprint of equal length. On the word 'GO' each player draws a line under the top line of print and then continues down the column from right to left and left to right under each line of print. The first person to reach the end of the column is the winner.

14 PING PONG FOOTBALL

Any age over 7 or 8 – 2 teams of 4 or more – Indoors – Equipment: ping pong ball.

Two teams are chosen and each have a goal at either end of the room. Then, getting down on their hands and knees, an ordinary ping pong ball is placed in the centre of the field of play and the players try to blow the ball to their opponents' goal. ONLY blowing is allowed. If the ball touches any part of a player's body, the other side gets a free blow from the centre of the field.

15 FEATHER FOOTBALL

Any age over 5 or 6 – Two teams of equal numbers – Indoors – Equipment: a feather, a long piece of tape or string.

Seat two teams on either side of a table, and mark a dividing line down the centre with the tape or string. Float the feather over the centre of the table and start the two teams blowing. If one team blows the feather over the edge of the table on the opposition's side, they collect two points. One point is earned if the feather lands on the table itself on the opposition's side. A match should constitute eleven points.

16 GUESSING GAMBLE

Any age over 5 or 6 – Any even number, in pairs – Indoors – Equipment: 5 small coins or buttons for each child.

This is a little bit of fun, juvenile gambling if you like, and can be organised on a knockout basis. Each person is given five small coins or buttons and places them in a pocket. Divide the competitors into pairs and stand them facing each other. Then each pair puts their hands into their pockets simultaneously and brings out so many of the objects. Placing their fists in front of each other, they must guess how many objects they have between them. The one nearest the correct number goes into the next round, and so on until you find an eventual winner.

17 SPOON BALLOON

Any age from 5 or 6 – Any number – Indoors – Equipment: large cardboard box, balloon and tablespoon for each player.

Place a large cardboard box at one end of the room. Line up the players as far as possible from the box and arm each one with a tablespoon. The idea is to balance the balloon on the spoon until it is safely in the box. If a player's balloon should touch the floor *en route* to the box then he must return to the starting line. The winner will be the first person to get his balloon in the box. See drawing.

11

18 HUNT THE KEY

Any age over 5 or 6 – Any number – Indoors – Equipment: a long piece of string, a latch key and, possibly, music.

Stand the players close together in a line holding a length of string on to which a latch key has been slipped, and choose one player to stand in front of the line as odd man out. Pass the key up and down the string without making the move too obvious. The odd man out calls 'STOP' and points to whoever he thinks is covering the key with his hand. This game can also be played to music. Follow the same procedure and when the music stops odd man out must try to find the key. If successful, then the key holder and the odd man out change places.

19 LIFT WRESTLE

Any age over 8 or 9 – 2 at a time – Outdoors – Equipment: none.

This is a knockout game for two people at a time. Each one must try to lift his opponent off the floor – and no holds barred, provided they are not violent. Both feet off the ground will give the 'lifter' victory.

20 SING DOWN YOUR NEIGHBOUR

Icebreaker – Any age from 6 or 7 – Any number – Indoors or outdoors – Equipment: none.

The first person sings the first line of a popular song – then points to someone else. The second person must sing the second line of the song and choose another person to sing the third line. Anyone who fails to sing the correct line drops out of the game – and the last surviving singer wins.

21 PENNY DROPPING

Any age from 4 – Any number – Indoors – Equipment: a bucket, water, a dime, and 6 pennies for each child.

This is a good game to keep younger children amused for half an hour or so. In a bucket, place a dime and cover it with about six inches of water. Each player is then given six pennies and takes a turn dropping them into the bucket. The object is to cover the dime with the pennies. First lucky player to do this wins the dime.

22 MATCH BUILDING

Any age over 9 or 10 – Any number – Indoors – Equipment: an empty bottle plus 2 dozen matches for each player.

Give each competitor two dozen used matches and an empty bottle. On the word 'GO' the players must lay the matches on the top of the bottle, and the first to balance all his matches is declared the winner.

23 MUSICAL CHAIRS

Any age over 5 or 6 – Any number – Indoors – Equipment: chairs (one fewer than the number of players) and some music.

Place some chairs – one fewer than the number of children taking part – in a row, alternately facing left and right. Start the music, and tell the children to move round the chairs till the music stops, when they must make a dive for a seat. Stop the music suddenly – and after the resulting chaos, one child will be 'out'. Take away a chair after each round till the winner sits triumphantly on the last chair. For younger children, use soft cushions on the floor instead of chairs.

24 MURDER IN THE DARK

Any age over 11 or 12 (young children may find it frightening) – Any number – Indoors – Equipment: As many slips of paper as there are players.

This is a word and deed game of great excitement. Drop as many folded slips of paper as there are players into a box. On one of the slips is marked a cross; on another a circle. The competitor who draws the circle is the detective, and the person who draws the cross the murderer. The murderer keeps his identity quiet while the detective makes his position known. All the players except the detective disperse throughout the house — with the lights turned off. The murderer quietly walks around the house placing his hands on an unsuspecting victim, saying 'You are dead'; then the victim screams and the murderer escapes. On hearing the scream the detective hurries to the scene of the crime, putting on the lights as he goes. Everyone except the murderer must remain completely still. After viewing the body and the position of the other people the detective calls everyone into a room and starts questioning them. Everyone must answer truthfully, except of course, the murderer, who no doubt will lie like mad. The detective is allowed only two guesses, and if he is unsuccessful then the murderer must announce himself and the papers go into the box again. This is, of course, a game of skill, and one where the faces of the players will nearly always give the game away.

25 AUNT SALLY

Any age over 6 or 7 – Any number – Outdoors (definitely) – Equipment: tin cans on boxes, plus 3 balls each, or 3 balls per team.

In the garden, set up a series of tin cans on the top of some boxes, and draw a line about twelve feet away. Line up the players and give them three soft balls each, and tell them to knock as many cans as possible off the boxes. Score one point per hit. The team with the most points wins. This game can really be played in a variety of ways, as a team, individually, or as an elimination competition.

26 MUSICAL ISLANDS

Any age over 5 or 6 — Any number — Indoors — Equipment: strong, old place mats, about half as many as there are competitors, and some music.

Place small mats or 'islands' on the floor around the room — about half as many islands as there are competitors. Music should be playing in the background, and when it stops the players must jump for the safety of the islands. Those getting themselves 'Wet Feet' — in other words, those with only one foot on the mat, leave the game. Your eventual winner will be the last child standing on a mat.

27 MUSICAL CHARGE

Small children — Any number — Indoors — Equipment: small objects (one less than the number of players), and music.

Place a pile of objects — one fewer than the number of competitors taking part — in the centre of the room. The players circle the objects, accompanied by some music. When the music stops, they must each dive and pick up an object. The unlucky one without anything drops out — so does another object before the game starts all over again.

28 THIRTY SECOND WALK

Any age over 8 or 9 — Any number — Indoors — Equipment: a watch for the timekeeper.

Stand the competitors at one end of the room and leave the way clear to the other end of the room. The idea is for the competitors to time themselves to walk from the one end of the room to the other end in exactly thirty seconds. All watches must be removed and any clocks covered. Those reaching the end before the time runs out are disqualified. The winner will be the one who touches the far wall at the time when the referee calls 'Thirty', or the person closest to the correct timing.

29 APPLE DUCKING

Any age over 6 or 7 — Any number — Outdoors — Equipment: a bucket of water, and one apple for each contestant.

Float as many apples as you like in a bucket of water. Each competitor must try to bite into one of the apples, and lift it clear of the water. Those successful are allowed to eat the apple.

30 SARDINES

Any age over 7 or 8 — Any number within reason — Indoors — Equipment: none.

One of the oldest party games in the book. The idea is so very simple. The whole house is the field of play. One player goes off to hide in a fairly large vacant place. The others set off to find him. When one of them is successful then that person hides with the other, making sure first of all that he is doing so unnoticed by the others. The last finder is the next seeker.

31 SLING

Any age over 5 or 6 — Any number — Indoors or outdoors — Equipment: a very large salad bowl and 3 pennies for each child.

Stand competitors about six feet away from the salad bowl armed with three pennies. On the word 'GO' the players must try to throw the coins into the bowl. This is not as easy as it would seem, so you should find the winner fairly easily.

32 SHOPPING

Any age over 6 or 7 — Any number — Indoors — Equipment: large variety of everyday commodities.

Hide a variety of everyday commodities around the room. Give the players a list of the hidden items and at the word 'GO' let them go off to find them. The child who finds the most is, of course, the winner.

33 VICTORY

Players over 6 or 7 (who can spell) — Number governed by number of cards (5 per child) — Indoors — Equipment: 2 packs of alphabet cards.

Scatter two packs of alphabet cards face downwards on a table and stand the players as far away from the table as possible. On the word 'Go' they dash to the table and pick up a card. The idea is to form a five-letter word, so each time they pick up a card that they don't want they must dash back to base, and then return to the table for another card. Players must not take more than one card at a time and each time they take a card they must return to base or be disqualified.

34 SWEET BAG DARTS

Any young children — Any number — Indoors — Equipment: 3 bags filled or partly filled with candy for each child, and 3 fairly large concentric rings cut out of cardboard or paper.

Place three rings of cardboard on the floor, one outside the other. The players stand about eight to ten yards away, each armed with three small bags filled with wrapped candy. They toss the bags in turn at the circles, and the child with the highest score wins. Score five points for the centre circle, three points for the middle circle, and one point for the outside circle. If the floor can take it, you can dispense with the rings and chalk out three circles instead.

35 MATCHBOX RELAY

Any age from 6–7 upwards — Even numbers (in pairs) — Indoors — Equipment: string, empty matchboxes, paper cups and some short sticks or garden canes.

Tie a piece of string about three feet long to each stick or cane, and then tie an empty matchbox to the other end of the string. Mark a 'starting line' and 'finishing line' at either end of the room with two long pieces of string. Stand a row of paper cups just in front of the starting line. Divide the players into pairs, one at each end of the room. Each player at the 'start' is handed a cane and, at the word 'GO', begins to knock his paper cup towards the 'finish' with the matchbox. His cup must go over the finishing line before his partner can take the cane and begin to knock the cup back towards the start. First one 'home' is the winner.

36 WOOLLY TANGLE

Any age over 5 or 6 — Any number — Indoors — Equipment: a chair entangled in wool for each child.

Place as many chairs as there are players and wind a ball of wool around the legs and backs of each chair. Seat the players, and on the

16

word 'GO' let the players roll the wool back into a ball. The first to wind the ball up – without breaking the wool – is the winner. For older players, you can make the game more difficult by stating that the players must remain seated.

37 SIX STEP BUFF

Any age over 6 or 7 – Any number – Indoors – Equipment: a blindfold.

This is a variation of the traditional game of Blind Man's Buff. Odd man out stands in the middle of the room, blindfolded. The others scatter and remain motionless. Odd man out twirls around three times and takes six paces forward. If he can touch anyone with outstretched hands, he then changes place with the one he has caught.

38 TREASURE HUNT

Any age over 5 or 6 — 2 teams of 10 or more — Indoors — Equipment: 30 pieces of white and 30 pieces of coloured paper.

Form two teams and give one team thirty pieces of white paper and the other team thirty pieces of coloured paper. Send the teams one at a time into a room to hide their pieces of paper. Better still, the host can hide the paper, but of course time is not always on the host's side. Anyway, once the paper has all been hidden, let the two teams begin the hunt. The first to find the thirty pieces of the opposing team's paper become the winners. For smaller numbers, reduce the number of pieces of paper.

17

39 HOT AND COLD CROSS

Teenagers or adults – Any number – Indoors – Equipment: none.

The players are seated with their arms folded and their legs crossed. The leader begins a rambling story, into which he weaves the words 'cheese' and 'crackers'. When he says 'cheese' the players must immediately unfold their arms and uncross their legs. When he says 'crackers' they must fold arms and cross legs. The last person to cross or uncross at the given word drops out of the game. The last player left in is the winner.

40 WORD DRILL

Players over 6 or 7 (able to spell) — 2 teams of 10 players — Indoors — Equipment: 2 alphabet cards for each player.

Form two teams of ten players, each player holding two alphabet cards. The referee then calls a word and it is up to the team to collect the letters making up the word. The first team to deliver the completed word to the referee collects one point. We suggest one game should equal five points and that the words should be short and simple.

41 WOOLLY NOLLY

Any age over 4 – 2 teams of about 6 players – Indoors – Equipment: plenty of scraps of different-coloured wools.

Scraps of wool in five different colours are scattered all over the room and on the word 'GO' the two teams of, say, six players each, must collect as many as possible. Score on a points system, say: RED five, BLUE four, GREEN three, YELLOW two, BROWN one. On the word 'STOP' the teams must return all collected wool and the umpire add up the score.

42 CIRCLE GAP

Any age over 6 or 7 – 2 teams of 6–8 players – Outdoors – Equipment: 2 beach balls.

The teams form two circles with one player in the middle of each. He throws a beach ball to Number One in the circle, who returns it, runs outside his neighbour, and catches the ball again at every gap right round the circle. When the first man returns home, Number Two sets off. The team to complete this operation first wins.

43 SILENT CELERY

Any age from 5 or 6 — Any number — Indoors & Equipment: Microphone if available (but this is not essential), celery or potato chips.

If you have a microphone this can be even more fun, but you can also play it easily if everyone keeps quiet. Small pieces of celery are handed to each contestant in turn, the rest of the party are judges and the person who manages to eat the celery with the least amount of noise is the winner. Nobody may vote for themselves. Potato chips may be used if no celery is available. No swallowing whole is allowed. The celery or potato chips *must* be chewed — for safety as well as fun.

44 JELLY THROUGH A STRAW

Any age over 6 or 7 — Any number — Indoors — Equipment: an individual jelly for each player, and some straws.

At the starting signal, each player must begin to eat his jelly by sucking it up through the straw. The first to succeed is the winner. The trick is to break the jelly up before you start.

45 DROP THE HANKIE

Any age over 5 or 6 — Any number — Outdoors if possible — Equipment: 1 handkerchief.

Players stand in a circle facing inwards, with the odd man out walking around the outside of the circle, and dropping a handkerchief behind someone in the circle as inconspicuously as possible. The person who finds the handkerchief behind him must pick it up and try to race the odd man out back to the place he has just left. If the odd man out loses, then he must continue as such until he beats a victim — who then himself becomes the odd man out.

46 MATCH-MAKING

Any age from 6 or 7 — Any number — Indoors — Equipment: several tin boxes containing used matches, paper clips, buttons etc.

Place eighty to a hundred used matches in a box, making note of how many. Do the same with paper clips, buttons and any other small objects. Place them on a table and let the children walk around and rattle them and estimate how many of each there are. The person with the nearest grand total is the winner, with a special prize for anyone who gets the exact number of any of the individual items correct. Remember, the items must not be taken out of the boxes.

47 WHO ARE THEY?

Any age from 12 or 13 — 2 teams of equal numbers — Indoors — Equipment: none.

The players are divided into two teams, and each player adopts the name of a famous person from the world of sport, the theatre, rock, or politics. Then two of one team conduct a conversation (in charac-

ter) without mentioning the name of their identity. They can discuss their vocation, age, successes, achievements, etc. Then the other team must guess who they are. If the guessers are correct they collect a point, and then two of their team perform. The team with the highest score wins.

48 YES AND NO

Any age from 7 or 8 – Any number of pairs – Indoors – Equipment: none.

Players pair off and take it in turns to question their opposite number who must not say 'Yes' or 'No'. The player that lasts out the longest will be the winner.

49 TRUE OR FALSE?

Any age from 9 or 10 – Any number of pairs – Indoors – Equipment: none.

This is a variation of 'Yes and No', and also for two people at a time. The first player makes a statement, and his partner must answer 'True' or 'False'. If the answer is correct, then the partner scores a point. Each pair asks each other six questions, and the partner with the most correct replies goes on to challenge the winners of the other pairs.

50 GIANT'S TREASURE

Any age over 5 or 6 — Any number — Indoors or outdoors — Equipment: a pile of cookies and candy.

One child takes the part of the 'giant' who lies guarding a pile of cookies and candy. The 'giant' pretends to be asleep and the other children try to steal the treasure. If he sits up they must stand completely still. If someone is caught moving after the 'giant' has sat up, he is out of the game. The first person to reach the treasure uncaught becomes the new 'giant'.

51 SECOND HAND SHOP

Any age from 5 or 6 — Any number — Indoors — Equipment: as many old clothes, shoes, etc. as possible.

Place as many clothes of all kinds that you can possibly find in the centre of the room. On the word 'GO' the children dash into the centre and put on as many garments as possible. At the word 'STOP' (say, two minutes later) count which player is wearing the most clothes from the pile. He or she is then announced as the winner. Suggested clothing: Shirts, trousers, pants, scarves, hats, socks, shoes, belts, ties, coats, overcoats, dresses, slips, jumpers, pullovers, cardigans, etc. See drawing.

52 WRONG LETTER

Teenagers or adults — Any number — Indoors — Equipment: none, but a dictionary might stop arguments !

Seat the players around in a circle and choose a word (for example: TELEVISION). The players then in order must call out a letter: thus, the leader calls 'T', and also says how many letters his word contains. The next person on his immediate right then should call 'E', the next player 'L' and so on. Each time a person calls a wrong letter, he or she must drop out. The last person left, or the person who completes a word, wins that round. If you decide that a series of words will cause more fun, then try the following: PHYSIOTHERAPY, PHYSIOLOGY, PHYSIOGRAPHY, PHYSIOGNOMY.

53 MISSING VOWEL

Players over 8 (who can spell) — Any number — Indoors — Equipment: a sheet of paper for each child, each containing the same clues, envelopes, and a pencil each.

Prepare fifteen to twenty words with the vowels omitted. For example. PL-Y-R (PLAYER); H-P- (HOPE); -LPH-B-T (ALPHABET) etc. Write the clues on a piece of paper, one sheet for each player, and seal them in envelopes. When you are ready to start, give each child an envelope and a pencil. On the word 'GO' let them start to fill in the missing vowels, thus making up the complete words After, say, sixty seconds, call a halt — and award a prize to the person who has the most words completed.

54 ARMLOCK WRESTLING

Boys over 7 or 8 — Any even number — Outdoors if possible — Equipment: none.

Two players sit back to back, feet astride and elbows interlocked. Each contestant tries to force his opponent's right shoulder to the ground.

55 MUSICAL MATES

Any age from 5 or 6 — Any number (in pairs) — Indoors — Equipment: chairs (one fewer than the number of pairs), and music.

People are paired off, boy/girl, etc, and chairs are lined up in a row, one fewer than the number of couples. The boys then parade around the row of chairs and the girls likewise in the opposite direction. Music is played and when it stops the boy must be seated with his original partner on his lap. The unlucky couple without a chair then drop out and a chair is removed. This procedure is followed until there is one couple left sitting on one chair.

56 TRAIN TAG

Small children (especially boys) – Any odd number – Indoors or outdoors – Equipment: none.

Players divide into pairs, with one person left as odd man out. One member of each pair is the engine, the second is the coach, and clasps his arms around the 'engine'. The 'trains' set off around the room and the odd man out tries to catch a train by putting his arms around the coach. When successful, the 'engine' drops out and becomes the odd man out and so on. A game really for the very young.

57 LONDON BRIDGE

Any age from about 4 – Any even number – Indoors or outdoors – Equipment: none.

Two players are chosen to be London Bridge. They face each other and join hands, holding their arms high in the air to form an arch. The rest of the players form a line and dance under the bridge and round in a large circle. Everybody sings the song and with the last words of every verse, the 'bridge' comes down and traps whoever is passing under the arch at the time. One member of the bridge is silver and the other gold. Each trapped player is asked which precious metal he chooses. He then lines up behind the appropriate side of the bridge. When all the players are sorted out into two teams, there is a tug-of-war.

Here are the verses from this famous old game.

1 London bridge is falling down,
   Falling down, falling down,
   London bridge is falling down,
   My fair lady.   (*Arms come down*)
2 Build it up with iron bars,
   Iron bars, Iron bars,
   Build it up with iron bars,
   My fair lady.   (*Arms come down*)
3 Iron bars will bend and break,
   Bend and break, bend and break,
   Iron bars will bend and break,
   My fair lady.   (*Arms come down*)
4 Build it up with pins and needles (etc) . . .
5 Pins and needles rust and bend . . .
6 Build it up with penny loaves . . .
7 Penny loaves will tumble down . .
8 Build it up with gold and silver . . .
9 Gold and silver I have not . . .
10 Here's a prisoner I have got . . .
11 What's the prisoner done to you . . .
12 Stole my watch and golden chain . . .

13 What will you take to set him free . . .
14 One hundred pounds will set him free . .
15 One hundred pounds we have not got . . .
16 Then off to prison he must go . . .

58 LOOBY LOO

Any age from about 4 – Any number – Indoors or outdoors – Equipment: none.

For this game all the players join hands in a circle and dance round singing the song and doing what the verses say.
Here is the song :

1 Here we dance Looby Loo   (*Circle skips to the right*)
Here we dance Looby Light   (*Circle skips to the left*)
Here we dance Looby Loo   (*Back to the right*)
On a Saturday night.   (*Back to the left*)
I put my right hand in   (*Players wave hand in circle*)
I put my right hand out
I give my right hand a shake
And turn myself about.

2 *Chorus* (Here we go Looby Loo, etc)
I put my left hand in
I put my left hand out,
I give my left hand a shake
And turn myself about.

3 *Chorus*
I put my two hands in . . .

4 *Chorus*
I put my right leg in . . .

5 *Chorus*
I put my left foot in . . .

6 *Chorus*
I put my right ear in . . .

7 *Chorus*
I put my left ear in . . .

8 *Chorus*
I put my whole self in . . .

59 LITTLE SALLY SAUCER

Small children – Any number – Indoors or outdoors – Equipment: none.

Players all form a circle and 'Sally' sits on the floor in the middle. Holding hands, the other players dance round her and sing while 'Sally' pretends to be crying.

Little Sally Saucer
Sitting in the water,
Weeping and crying,
Rise, Sally, rise.   (*'Sally' now stands up*)
Wipe off your eyes   (*'Sally' puts her hands over her eyes*)
Turn to the East   (*She turns one way with eyes closed*)
Turn to the West   (*She turns the other way*)
Now turn to one   (*With her eyes still closed,
You love the best.   'Sally' points to one of the
                          players in the circle*)

The person 'Sally' points at changes places and becomes the next 'Sally'. The game continues exactly as before.

60 A-HUNTING WE WILL GO

Small children — Any number — Indoors or outdoors — Equipment: none.

One player is chosen to be the 'Fox' and two others are the 'Lambs'. The rest of the players join hands in a circle around the 'Fox' and skip around him while singing. The 'Lambs' stay outside the circle.

A-Hunting we will go
A-Hunting we will go,
We'll catch a fox
And put him in a box,
And never let him go.

While the singing is going on, the 'Lambs' come close to the circle and tease the 'Fox', who tries to break out of the circle of players to catch them. The 'Lambs' have one safe place (perhaps against the furthest wall in the room, or by a tree), where the 'Fox' can't catch them. If the 'Fox' breaks out of the circle they run for safety, but if caught, the 'Lambs' become 'Foxes' and one player from the circle becomes another 'Lamb'.

61 THE MUFFIN MAN

Any age from about 4 — Any number — Indoors or outdoors — Equipment: none.

All players form a circle around a person in the middle. They dance round to the left and sing the first verse of the song.

Oh, do you know the muffin man,
The muffin man, the muffin man,
Oh, do you know the muffin man,
Who lives in Drury Lane?

Then the player in the middle dances round to the right and sings the answer.

Oh, yes I know the muffin man,
The muffin man, the muffin man,
Oh, yes I know the muffin man
He lives in Drury Lane.

The player in the middle then chooses a **partner** from the circle and the two join hands. The circle dances round again, repeating the first verse. For the second verse, the two in the middle sing:

Now TWO of us know the muffin man
(etc).

The two players choose a third and the game goes on until all the players in the outside circle have been brought in to the inside circle. Then they sing the last verse:

Now ALL of us know the muffin man
(etc).

62 A-TISKET, A-TASKET

Any age over 4 – Any number – Indoors or outdoors – Equipment: a handkerchief or small scarf.

All players join hands and form a big circle. One player is 'It' and carries a handkerchief or small scarf. 'It' runs around the circle singing and the other players sing too.

A-Tisket, A-Tasket,
A green and yellow basket,
I sent a letter to my love,
And on the way I dropped it.

I dropped it, I dropped it,
And on the way I dropped it.
Somebody here has picked it up,
And put it in their pocket.
It isn't you,
It isn't you,
IT'S YOU.

When 'It' shouts 'It's You', he drops the handkerchief right behind a player and starts running round the outside of the circle. The selected player picks up the handkerchief and runs in the opposite direction round the *inside* of the circle. The first person to reach the vacant space is safe, and whoever is left out is 'It' for the next game.

63 THE FARMER'S IN HIS DEN

Any age over 4 – Any number – Indoors or outdoors – Equipment: none.

Select one child to play the part of the farmer, and stand him in the middle of a circle formed by the other children. The circle then join hands and walk around the farmer singing:
    The farmer's in his den
    The farmer's in his den
    Heigh-ho heigh-ho
    The farmer's in his den.
The circle stops, and the farmer chooses one player to become his 'wife'. The circle then continues to walk around and starts singing:
    The wife wants a child
    The wife wants a child
    Heigh-ho heigh-ho
    The wife wants a child.
The wife then chooses someone to be her 'child' and the same operation continues. Followed by:
    The child wants a nurse
    The child wants a nurse
    Heigh-ho heigh-ho
    The child wants a nurse.
They then sing The nurse wants a dog etc, and finish with, We all pat the dog etc. Everyone then pats the dog who then becomes the farmer.

64 JINGLE BONNET

Any age over 4 – Any number – Indoors – Equipment: a hat and a good supply of pennies.

Each child places a penny in a hat, then, one after another, turns the hat upside down. The player who turns up the most heads wins all the pennies. It is surprising, but there is not usually a lot of money changing hands. See drawing.

65 HOT RICE

Any age over 5 or 6 — Any number — Indoors or outdoors — Equipment: small paper bag containing candy.

The odd man out dodges about in the centre of a circle of players trying to avoid being hit below the waist by a small paper bag of candy which is thrown by the players in the circle. The successful thrower then becomes odd man out.

66 FANNING THE KIPPER

Any age from 5 or 6 — Any number — Indoors — Equipment: tissue paper 'fishes', and a magazine for each child.

Cut out a number of fish shapes from tissue paper, and place them along a starting line. Give each competitor a magazine and stand them behind a fish. On the word 'GO' the competitors start fanning the fish to make them 'flap' to the finish at the other end of the room. Anyone touching the fish with the paper is disqualified and the first player to get his fish 'home'.wins. See drawing.

67 ELECTRIC SHOCK

Any age over 5 or 6 — Any even number — Indoors or outdoors — Equipment: none.

Divide the players into two equal teams and line them up behind two leaders. At a starting signal, the end player in each team claps his hand upon the shoulder of the person in front of him. As the second player feels the hand on his shoulder, he does the same to the third player, and so on. When the front member of each team feels the hand on his shoulder, he shouts 'Ouch' . . . showing that the circuit has been completed and he has felt the 'electric shock'. The first team to finish wins. After each game, the players in both teams change their order.

68 HOT AND COLD

Small children — Any number — Indoors — Equipment: 1 thimble or similar small object.

One player leaves the room. While he is away, the rest of the players hide a small object, such as a thimble, somewhere in the room. Then the odd man out comes in and must find the hidden object. He moves around only one step at a time in any direction. He then asks if he is warm, hot or cold. If he is near the object, he is 'Warm'. The nearer he gets to its hiding place the 'Hotter' he becomes. If he starts to move away from the hidden object he is getting 'Colder'. When he is 'Boiling' he is right by the place where the object is hidden.

69 HUMMING BIRDS

Small children — Any number — Indoors — Equipment: 1 thimble or similar small object.

This is a variation of 'Hot and Cold' which young children seem to enjoy. The rules are exactly the same except that instead of being told whether he is 'Hot or Cold', everyone else in the room hums loudly or softly according to how near the player is to the hidden object.

70 PAIR THE SOCKS

Any age over 5 or 6 — Any even number — Indoors — Equipment: lots of socks.

Get as many old clean men's socks as possible, of different colours and patterns, and mix them up. Each team is timed in turn pairing them with their backs to the pile — no turning round allowed. Each seated (and the floor is the best place) team member may reach for only one sock at a time and hold it in front to see if it makes a pair with anyone else's. If it does not it must be returned, without turning, to the pile. If it pairs it is put together with its partner in front of the team. The other team meanwhile helps or hinders by keeping the pile (which the pairing team cannot see) well mixed up and maybe adding an odd sock or two. The captain of the pairing team may choose to call out 'Now' to get his team reaching for extra socks

together so that the chance of pairing will be greater. Quickest team wins.

71 SHADOW CHASE

Any age over 4 – Any number – Outdoors on a sunny day – Equipment: none.

This is strictly an outdoor game for the garden lawn, and can only be played on fine sunny days. The reason is that it is a catch game ... but 'It' has to catch not the player, but his shadow. 'It' chases the other people around and tries to step on a shadow. When he manages this, he calls out the name of the person he has caught, who then becomes the next 'It'.

72 CRYPTIC CODES

Any age over 9 or 10 – Any number – Indoors – Equipment: pencil and paper for each child.

A quick pencil and paper game this – and a judge can stand by to hand out a small prize to the winner. All players must make up a sentence or phrase using only numbers, letters or symbols. The most original or amusing wins the prize.

Here are some examples, having made it a bit easier by allowing two normal words in each phrase.

U R	(You Are)
2 Good	(Too Good)
2 B	(To Be)
4 Got 10	(Forgotten)
R & T	(Auntie)
May C's	(Maisie's)
9 T 4	(Ninety-four)
2 Day	(Today)

73 SONG SCRAMBLE

Age can vary, according to which songs are chosen. — Any number — Indoors — Equipment: complete choruses of well-known songs, each line written separately on a slip of paper.

On separate slips of paper, write one line from the choruses of several popular songs. Each chorus-line must be completely written out. Every player is given two slips from a hat and they must swap between themselves until they have two consecutive lines. Then they must team up with one or more of the other players until they have the complete words of the song. You'll be surprised how difficult it is to recognise odd lines from even very well-known songs.

74 TOSS THE PROVERB

Any age over 9 or 10 – Any number – Indoors – Equipment: 1 ball.

All the players sit in a circle and one is given a ball. He has to recite a proverb – any proverb – then toss the ball to another player. Upon catching it, this player must also quickly recite a proverb before throwing the ball on to someone else. As you can see, this game becomes progressively more difficult as no proverb can be used more than once. As players fail to think up new proverbs, they drop out of the game.

75 CAPITALS

Any age over 9 or 10 – Any number – Indoors – Equipment: 1 ball.

The game is played exactly like 'Toss the Proverb' except that players must name a capital city whenever they catch the ball. If the game runs out of capitals too quickly, this may be extended to cover all cities (as distinct from towns).

76 KNOW YOUR PAPER

Teenagers or adults – Any number – Indoors – Equipment: a selection of national newspapers, scissors.

Cut a square from each newspaper and number the back so that you can tell which is which. Players have to identify each paper from the appearance of the type. This is not as difficult as it seems.

77 FISH POND

Icebreaker – Any age (especially round 8 or 9) – Indoors – Equipment: a pencil tied to a long piece of string for every boy.

This little game is very useful in pairing people off to be partners for dancing or for partner games. All the girls go outside a door, leaving it open just a couple of inches. Then each boy takes turns to throw a pencil tied to a long length of string over the top of the door. On the other side, a girl catches the pencil and her new partner 'reels in' his catch.

78 CUP CAPERS

Any age over 6 or 7 – Any number – Indoors – Equipment: some paper cups and plates.

Place a row of paper plates at one end of the room and line the players up about six feet away from the plates. Each player is given a paper cup which he balances on one of his feet. He must then try to walk to a plate and put the cup on it. It helps to take your shoes off for this one !

31

79 WHO AM I?

Any age over 8 or 9 — Any number — Indoors — Equipment: slips of paper with the names of famous people written on them — 1 for each player — and pins.

One judge is appointed and writes the names of several famous people (living or dead) upon separate slips of paper. Then each player has one of the names pinned to his back. Each player can then see what name everyone else has, but not his own. The object of the game is for each player to find out what name he carries on his back . . . and to do this he can ask any questions he likes of other players. Only 'Yes' or 'No' answers may be given. When each player thinks he knows who he is, he goes to the judge and makes a guess. He is allowed only three guesses.

One special point: Before playing this game, all mirrors should be covered up or removed.

80 MUSICAL SPOONS

Any age over 4 — Any number — Indoors — Equipment: some spoons (1 less than the number of players), radio or record-player.

A version of Musical Chairs which is ideal for younger children and useful if you haven't enough space to set out chairs. Spread out a number of spoons on the floor (one less than the number of players) and parade the players round in a circle in time to music. When the music stops, the players dive for a spoon, and the person without one leaves the game. Another spoon is removed, and the music begins again. The winner will be the person holding the very last spoon.

81 PING PONG FUN

Any age over 5 or 6 — Any number around 12 — Indoors — Equipment: 1 jam jar each, 2 wrapped candies each, and 1 table tennis ball each.

Place on a table (or on the floor) a dozen jam jars or so, and in each one put a couple of wrapped sweets. Stand the children about six to eight feet away and give them a table tennis ball. The idea is to throw the ball into the jars. Those successful win the candies.

82 BALL TACKLING

Any age over 6 or 7 — Any number — Outdoors — Equipment: 1 beach ball.

Players form a ring and pass a beach ball backwards and forwards over and across the circle. There are two odd men out in the circle and they must try to intercept the ball. When successful, the odd man out takes the place of the person in the circle who last touched the ball.

83 STEPS TO LONDON

Any age from 5–6 — Any number — Indoors — Equipment: none.

One person stands with his back to the others, who go to the other end of the room. Everyone creeps towards him, with the intention of touching him before he catches them moving. Whenever he feels inspired the odd man out twirls round, and whoever he sees moving drops out. The player who succeeds in touching odd man out takes his place.

84 FAMILY PROJECTOR FUN

Teenagers or adults — Any number — Indoors — Equipment: a film projector, slides, a list of place names and a pencil for each player.

Each player is given a list of place names and a pencil. The slides of places are then run through the projector in any order, either upside down or very, very quickly. The player who comes nearest to marking his list with the order in which the slides were shown wins the game.

85 FAMOUS NAMES

Any age over 9 or 10 — Any number — Indoors — Equipment: a list of well-known people.

Compile a list of well-known names, and divide the children into two teams. Then call out the last name of, say, a sporting personality, followed by a rock singer and so on. The idea is for the children to call back the first name, two points going to the team with the correct answer. Twenty-one answered questions constitutes a game.

86 LOOP THE LOOP

Icebreaker – Teenagers or adults – Any number of pairs – Indoors – Equipment: a 4 foot piece of string for each player.

A little preparation is needed for this party game. You will need a long piece of string (about four feet) for every player. The leader sorts everyone into pairs. Then, taking the first person, he ties one end of the string to one wrist and the other end to the other wrist. Then, taking another piece of string, he loops this through the tied person's arms and then ties each end of the second piece on to his partner's wrists. Thus the two people are tied loosely together with several feet of string.

The leader ties every pair up in the same way, and then announces the start of the game – which is to find the first pair who can unlink themselves without breaking or untying the string. The resulting antics will send everyone into fits of laughter.

Note: It is a wise precaution to ask anyone who knows the trick of this game to keep quiet about it. The reason for this is simple; the thing is completely impossible. But usually people twist themselves in knots before they realise that you just cannot separate two linked circles.

87 WHY WHEN AND WHERE

Any age over 8 or 9 — Any number — Indoors — Equipment: none.

'Why, When and Where' is a guessing game that keeps several people stimulated at the same time. 'It' is chosen and leaves the room while the others think of a noun. 'It' then comes back and must guess the noun by asking only three types of question. However, he may ask as many questions as he likes so long as they are of the same type.

For example, suppose the word chosen was 'Pencil'.

'It' will ask: '*Why* is this object useful?'

Someone answers: 'Because it leaves an impression.'

'It' then asks: '*When* can you use it?'

Someone answers: 'Anytime is always the right (write) time.'

'It' asks: '*Where* do you use it?'

Someone answers: 'On paper.'

This last answer was not as cryptic or clever as the others, so 'It' might guess 'Pencil'. If not, he asks other 'Why, When and Where' questions until he knows the answer.

88 TWENTY QUESTIONS

Any age from 8 to 80 — Any number — Indoors — Equipment: none, but a question-master is necessary.

Popular as a party game and as a long-running radio and television series, Twenty Questions has been with us for years . . . and most people still enjoy playing it. Each player thinks of something which is either animal, vegetable or mineral. This is the only clue he gives the rest of the players, who then have a total of 20 questions in which to discover the nature of the object. Clever players at this game work by a process of elimination and note carefully the answers to previous questions.

89 PIXILLATED PROVERBS

Teenagers and over — Any number — Indoors — Equipment: none.

Every player thinks of a well-known proverb, or a famous advertising slogan, and rephrases it into something unusual which means more or less the same thing. Then other players must guess the original proverb.

Here are some examples of how this might work:

(1) 'Look before you leap' might be rephrased as: 'It is highly desirable to survey the terrain before making a rapid forward motion'.

(2) 'A duplication of culinary experts causes damage to the finished product'. Get that one? It's our old favourite: 'Too many cooks spoil the broth'.

(3) 'A stitch in time saves nine' might become: 'A simple movement with a needle and thread may save less than ten people'.

Everyone in the room must have a turn at this game.

90 HINK PINK

Icebreaker — All the family and guests over 6 or 7 — Any number — Indoors — Equipment: none.

Nobody wins or loses in this game, but it's a good laughter-raiser and fun for everyone in the family. Everyone tries to think of a pair of amusing, odd and rhyming words. Then players in turn announce that they have a 'HINK PINK' and give a clue as to what it is.

For instance, someone might think of 'Stout Trout', so he would say: 'My Hink Pink is a fat fish'.

Someone else thinks of 'Fat Cat', so announces that his 'Hink Pink is well-fed and furry'.

For two-syllable words, such as 'Bony Pony' or 'Hairy Fairy' the player says 'Hinkie Pinkie'. For three-syllable words, he would say 'Hinketty Pinketty'.

As each player thinks of his rhyme, he gives everyone a chance to guess what it is before telling them the answer.

91 DOWN YOU GO

Any age over 8 or 9 — Any number — Indoors — Equipment: blackboard or large sheet of paper, and chalk (or thick pencil).

For this game you need a blackboard or a large sheet of paper. The leader writes dashes upon the board to represent a well-known phrase. Suppose, for example, the phrase were 'Bacon and Eggs', then the leader would write – – – – – – – – – – – –

A simple clue is given to start the game off. In this case, the leader might say: 'You eat it'.

Then the other players take it in turns to call out a letter of the alphabet. If the letter belongs in the phrase, the leader marks it in and the player gets a point. If, however, the letter does not belong in the phrase, the player is out. The player who guesses the finished phrase gets five bonus points.

92 LEMON ROLL

Any age over 6 or 7 — Any even number — Indoors — Equipment: 2 lemons and 2 pencils (plus a few spares just in case).

Ever tried to roll a lemon across the floor using the pointed end of a pencil? Well, this game gives everyone a chance to see how difficult it can be. Form two teams with the players lined up behind one another. On the starting signal the first player of each team tries to poke his lemon across the room and back with a pencil. Then the second team member repeats the procedure and the relay game goes on until one complete team has finished the course.

93 ORANGES AND LEMONS

Any age over 4 – Any even number – Indoors or outdoors (you need plenty of room) – Equipment: none.

Choose two people to hold hands and form an arch, one of them to be known as 'oranges' and the other as 'lemons'. The other players then form a chain and march under the arch singing:

      'Oranges and Lemons', say the Bells of St. Clement's;
      'You owe me five farthings,' say the Bells of St. Martin's;
      'When will you pay me ?' say the Bells of Old Bailey;
      'When I grow rich,' say the Bells of Shoreditch;
      'When will that be ?' say the Bells of Stepney;
      'I'm sure I don't know,' say the Great Bells of Bow;
      'Well . . . here comes a candle to light you to bed
      'And here comes a chopper to chop off your head,
      'So chop ! chop ! the last man's head . . .'

At the words 'The last man's head' the arch makes a chopping motion and catches one of the children. The 'prisoner' is then asked to stand behind the member of the arch with the name of her choice, either 'oranges' or 'lemons'. When all the children have been caught the two teams have a tug-of-war.

94 ADVERBS

Any age over 6 or 7 – Any number – Indoors – Equipment: none.

'It' leaves the room while the other players choose an adverb. The more unusual the adverb, the more fun the game. Then 'It' comes in and asks players in turn to act out certain things 'in the manner of the adverb'. Each player must perform a little act and 'It' tries to guess the word. Suppose the word were 'Boisterously', then 'It' might ask someone to eat in the manner of the adverb, and the resultant mime could be very amusing.

95 STOOP AND STAND

Any age from about 5 – Any number – Indoors or outdoors – Equipment: none.

Players arrange themselves in a circle round the leader. The leader calls out 'I say stoop' and bends over. All players must follow suit. Then the leader stands upright and says: 'I say stand'. Once again, all the players must follow.

Then the leader tries to trick everyone. He may call out: 'I say stoop' and remain in a standing position. The trick of the game is doing exactly what the leader DOES, not what he SAYS Anyone who is wrong is sent out of the game – and the faster it is played, the more fun it is.

96 HOP AND TIP

Any age from about 5 – Any even number – Indoors or outdoors – Equipment: none.

Players arrange themselves into two teams, facing each other. The first players of each team stand on one leg and hop towards each other. Then, by no more than slapping hands together, each player must force his opponent to lose balance and place the other foot on the ground. The winner goes back to stand in his team and the loser leaves the game completely. When each player has had a turn, the team with the most members remaining wins the game.

97 CHARLIE TAG

Small children – Any number – Indoors or outdoors – Equipment: none, but someone must know the rhyme to get the game going.

Players form a circle round the 'Charlie' and hold hands. They then chant the following little rhyme:
> Charlie over the water
> Charlie over the sea
> Charlie caught a great big fish
> But Charlie can't catch me.

38

As soon as the song is finished, all players must quickly bend down to place both hands on the floor. 'Charlie' must catch someone before they have placed both hands down. If he succeeds, that player becomes the next 'Charlie'.

98 HERE WE COME GATHERING NUTS IN MAY

Small children – Any number – Indoors or outdoors – Equipment: 1 large handkerchief.

This game can be played by both boys and girls, indoors and outdoors. The players form two equal teams facing each other, with a handkerchief placed to show the centre. One side joins hands and walks up to the centre and back singing:

'Here we come gathering nuts in May, nuts in May, nuts in May
Here we come gathering nuts in May, on a cold and frosty morning.'

The other side then joins hands and walks up to the centre and back singing:

'Whom will you have for nuts in May, nuts in May, nuts in May,
Whom will you have for nuts in May, on a cold and frosty morning?'

The first side then says who it will have, and advancing and retreating again sings:

'We will have ——— for nuts in May, nuts in May, nuts in May,
We will have ——— for nuts in May on a cold and frosty morning.'

The other side then sings:

'And whom will you have to fetch her (him) away, fetch her away, fetch her away,
And whom will you have to fetch her away on a cold and frosty morning?'

The first team then chooses someone from its own line and sings:

'We'll send ——— to fetch her away', etc.

The two chosen players then have a tug-of-war with a handkerchief, and the loser joins the winner's side. The game goes on until one side has no players left.

99 AUTOGRAPHS

Any age over 7 or 8 – Any number – Indoors – Equipment: pencils and paper for each child.

Every player is given a pencil and a sheet of paper. Then a leader gives each contestant a slip of paper bearing a famous name. The object of the game is for each player to compile a complete list of all the names – and to do this he must collect the signature of every other 'famous person'. The first player with a complete set of 'autographs' wins.

100 BROOMSTICK

Any age over 6 or 7 – Any number – Indoors – Equipment: a broom.

You need a large room for this game, which is a more boisterous version of Catch the Cane. You will also need a broom.

One player stands in the middle of the room, and holds the broom upside down on the floor. Then he calls out the name of another player, lets go of the broom and runs away. The player whose name is called must grab the broom before it hits the ground, then name someone else to catch it. Anyone who does not reach the broom before it hits the floor goes out of the game.

This game is best played very quickly, and with all players kept as far away from the broom as possible. If the room is large, you may make it a rule that every player must be touching one of the walls when the broomstick is being held.

101 DEER HUNT

Any age over 6 or 7 – Any number, 2 at a time – Indoors – Equip-ment: 2 blindfolds.

This game is played by two people at a time, but others will enjoy just watching the fun. Two players are chosen to be the deer and the hunter. Both are blindfolded and placed at opposite sides of a large table or a circle of chairs. The hunter has to catch the deer, and to do this must creep quietly around. Both hunter and deer can make noises to confuse each other – for instance the deer might make a noise from one side of the table then quickly move round to the other. When the hunter eventually catches the deer, two other players take over.

102 BALL BOUNCING RELAY

Any age over 6 or 7 – 2 teams of 4 to 8 players – Outdoors – Equipment: 2 beach balls.

Line up two teams of between four to eight players and give the first member in each team a beach ball. He bounces the ball to the player on his left, the next player does the same, and so on, until the ball reaches the end of the line. When the last person in the line receives the ball, he then bounces it back to the person on his right and so on back to the start. The first team to bounce the ball up and down the line are the winners. If a ball is grounded then the team must start all over again. The game can also be played with the players seated. See drawing.

103 ANIMALS

Any age over 6–7 – Any even number – Indoors or outdoors – Equipment: pencils and paper for each player.

Players are sorted out into two teams and everyone is given a pencil and a piece of paper. Then the first team decides upon a type of animal for every member in the team. When they have chosen their animals, both teams walk up to each other and the opposing members ask six questions of their opposite number.

Nobody may ask a direct question, such as: 'What animal are you?' They can, for example, ask: 'Are you big or small?', 'Are you furry or smooth?', 'Do you eat meat or do you eat grass?' and so on.

When the six questions have been asked, the opposing team must write down all the animals they think they have guessed. Then it is their turn to be animals and give the first team six guesses. The team with the most right wins the game. Lots of fun is added to this game by having all the players close together in two lines. Everyone is talking at once, and the situation can become very mixed up.

104 LUCKY NUMBERS

Any age over 5 – Any number – Indoors or outdoors – Equipment: 5 buttons for every child.

This is a nice little game for giving small prizes, like bars of chocolate or sweets. Everyone is given five buttons to hold. Then they all move from player to player for a minute, giving away as many buttons as they like to anyone. No player may refuse to accept any number of buttons he is offered.

Every now and again, the leader calls 'Stop' and then calls out a number between one and twenty. Any player who holds that number of buttons receives a prize.

105 FEATHER BLOWING

Any age over 6 or 7 – Any number – Indoors – Equipment: a feather.

Huddle the guests close together in the centre of the room and throw the feather in the air above them. The idea is then quite simple. Everyone must blow like mad at the feather to stop it touching them. Anyone who is touched by the feather falls out, until there is an eventual winner. This is a great game for youngsters who have 'the gift of the gab'. It certainly leaves them short of breath. See drawing.

106 MARKET

Any age over 6 or 7 – Any number – Indoors – Equipment: none.

This is a word game which is a test of memory as well. The first players says: 'Farmer Jones went to market and bought a pig'. The second player says: 'Farmer Jones went to market and bought a pig and a bunch of grapes'. The third player says: 'Farmer Jones went to market and bought a pig, a bunch of grapes and a toy trumpet'. The fourth player says: 'Farmer Jones went to market and bought a pig, a bunch of grapes, a toy trumpet and a ball of string'. The fifth player will probably say: 'Help, I've forgotten'. So he's out and the game continues. One new item must be added each time.

107 WHAT'S YOUR TRADE?

Any age over 9 or 10 – Two teams of up to 10 players – Indoors or outdoors – Equipment: none.

Two teams of up to ten players can take part in this game, which needs a large room (or a garden). The two teams are both given a 'safety area' on opposite sides of the room. This area is plainly marked off. The first team must quietly agree on a certain trade or profession. When they have done so, they walk in a line from their safety area into the half-way mark between the two safety areas. Both teams then chant the following little rhyme:

First Team: 'Here we come.'
Second Team: 'Where from?'
First Team: 'Home from work. We never shirk.'
Second Team: 'What's your trade?'
First Team: 'Lemonade.'
Second Team: 'Give us some.'
First Team: 'If you can run.'

Then the first team call out the initials of their chosen trade and act it out in pantomime. For instance, if they had chosen the trade of Dog-Catcher, they would call out the initials D.C. and some might act like wild dogs, while others pretend to chase and catch them. The second team now have five chances at guessing the job or trade. If they are successful, the first team must make a sudden break back to their

safety area. The second team give chase and if they catch any players before they reach safety, those players become members of the opposite team. Each team takes it in turn to choose a trade and the game goes on until one team has all the players.

108 PING PONG RACE

Any age over 5 – Any number – Outdoors – Equipment: a dessert spoon and table tennis ball for each child.

This can be a very amusing version of the Egg and Spoon race. Line up the players at the starting line, equipped with a dessert spoon and a table tennis ball. Prepare a track, say, from one end of the lawn to the other. On the word 'GO' the players put the ball in the spoon and trot off. First across the finishing line is the winner. If anyone drops the ball or is caught holding it he must go back to the start.

109 PAPER RIPPING

Any age over 8 or 9 – Any number, but about 6 at a time – Indoors – Equipment: a pile of pages from magazines.

This game is best played by no more than six children at a time. Give each child a page from a magazine and on the word 'GO' call out a number – say, 15. The first child to bring you fifteen pieces of the magazine page is the winner. There must not be any pieces of the page left over.

110 PUSH FOOTBALL

Any age over 7 or 8 – Two teams of 5 players – Outdoors – Equipment: two sets of 'goal posts' or markers (almost anything will do) and a large ball.

Put a set of goal posts or markers at either end of the lawn and pick two teams of five players: one goalkeeper, two full backs and two forwards.

To play the game the players must remain in either a kneeling or crouching position and must not stand up. The idea is to push the ball around – either with the palm of the hand or the fist. Standing up, pulling an opponent's shirt, or (even worse!) pushing your opponent over, constitutes a foul and the offender is automatically sent off. The game can be played either as a five minute each way session or the best of five goals.

111 FORBIDDEN WORDS

Any age over 7 or 8 – Any number – Indoors or outdoors – Equipment: none.

Any number of players sit in a circle – either on chairs or on the floor. One person is chosen to be the leader and he chooses certain words which must not be said. 'Yes' and 'No' must always be forbidden words – and any others the leader chooses. The leader then asks any player a question. The player must answer at once, without using any of the forbidden words. The leader tries to trick everyone into using the words – and if they do, they are out of the game. The last surviving player is the winner and becomes the next leader.

112 BLOW FOOTBALL

Any age over 7 or 8 – Two teams of 4 – Indoors – Equipment: something to act as goals, drinking straws and a table tennis ball.

Mark a table with two goals about eight inches apart. Equip four players on either side of the table with a drinking straw each and place a table tennis ball in the centre. On the word 'GO' the eight players start blowing until someone scores. You need to be a good referee to keep this game in order! Fouls are not permitted and if any member of a team tries to move over to the opponent's side of the table he will automatically be 'sent off'.

113 FRENCH CRICKET

Any age over 6 or 7 – 2 teams of 4 – Outdoors – Equipment: cricket bat and tennis ball.

All you need for this game is a cricket bat, a tennis ball, and two teams of four boys or girls. The side batting must place their players in batting order and the opening batsman takes his stance, standing with his feet together and the cricket bat in front of his legs. The opposition must then try to 'bowl him out' by hitting his legs with the ball. If successful, then the next opposing batsman comes in. Every time the batsman deflects the ball his team scores one run. When all the batsmen are 'out', the teams change over. The four totals of each team are added together for the final score.

114 BLOW THE CUP RELAY

Any age – Any even number – Indoors – Equipment: 2 plastic or paper cups, twine or thread.

A little preparation is needed for this team game, but the fun makes it well worth the trouble. You will need two plastic or paper drinking cups and plenty of garden twine or strong thread.

   Stretch two lines of twine across the room, and thread one end through a small hole in the bottom of the cup. Each cup should move easily on the twine. Tie the ends of the twine to sturdy furniture, and choose two teams to line up at one end of the room. The first player of each team must *blow* the paper cup to the other end of the twine. When he reaches the end, he slides it back with his hand and the next player in the team begins. The first team to complete the course will be out of breath, but they will have won the game. See drawing.

115 FIRE ALARM

Any age over 6 or 7 — Any number — Indoors — Equipment: 1 alarm clock.

While all the players go out of the room, a grown-up hides an alarm clock somewhere — having already set it to go off in exactly five minutes. When the clock is hidden, the players enter the room and try to find it.

When someone finds the clock, he pretends not to notice it — because he doesn't want anyone else to know his secret. Instead, he play-acts for a few seconds, then just walks out of the room again. When the alarm goes off, any players still looking for the clock are out of the game. The whole house can be used for this game, and the clock re-wound until one last winner is found.

116 DOTTY DRAWINGS

Any age — Any number — Indoors — Equipment: paper and pencils.

Each player is given a pencil and a clean sheet of paper, and has to make six dots anywhere on the paper. Then each player exchanges his sheet of paper with someone else. The second part of the game is for everyone to make some sort of picture by joining the dots into a recognisable object or person. The funniest or most ingenious drawing wins, and a prize can be given.

117 BLIND ARTIST

Any age — Any number — Indoors — Equipment: blindfold, paper, pencils.

Everyone is given a pencil and a sheet of paper. Each player in turn is blindfolded and told to draw a certain object or animal. After everyone has had a turn, the pictures are compared and the funniest or cleverest picture wins a prize.

118 MAD MONSTERS

Any age — Any number — Indoors — Equipment: pencils and paper.

Give a pencil and strips of paper about six inches long to each player. Tell everyone to draw the head of a person, an animal or a bird, leaving a couple of small lines for the next player to join on to before folding the paper so that the drawing of the head is hidden. The slips are then passed round clockwise and the next person draws a body. One more fold, and the slips are passed on again for someone else to draw legs. When the slips are unfolded, there will be some pretty strange monsters.

46

119 TEASPOON AND SUGAR CUBE RACE

Icebreaker — Any age over 6 or 7 — 2 teams of 5-10 players — Indoors — Equipment: 1 teaspoon and 2 sugar cubes for each player.

Players are sorted into two teams and each player is given a teaspoon. The teams line up side by side and a sugar cube is placed in the teaspoon of the leader of each team. Holding the teaspoon in their mouths, the leaders tip the sugar into the next player's spoon (also held in the mouth) and pass it on down the line. If the sugar cube is dropped, the game goes back to the first player. The first team to pass the sugar completely down the line wins the game.

120 STRAW AND DISC RACE

Any age over 7 — Any even number — Indoors — Equipment: drinking straws and 12 coloured paper discs.

Another good team game for any number of players. The materials you need are drinking straws for each player, and twelve small discs cut from coloured paper. The team leaders are given six discs each. The object of the game is to pass all six discs right down the line using only the straws. This can be done by placing the end of the straw over the paper disc and sucking in to hold it in position. The tricky bit comes when the next person has to take the disc from the end of the straw without letting it drop to the ground. See drawing.

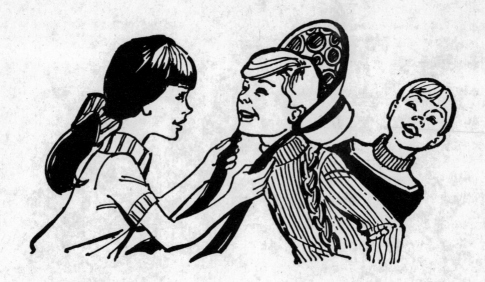

121 BONNET RACE

*Any age over 5 – Any number, in 2 teams – Indoors or outdoors –
Equipment: two old hats with sewn-on ribbons.*

Line up two teams and hand the first member in each team a bonnet.
The first child places the bonnet on his head, and ties the bow under
the chin. He then turns round to face the next member of the team,
who undoes the bonnet, places it on his own head, ties the bow, and
turns to the next player in the line. The winning team will be the one
that finishes first !

122 PLACE THE FACE

*For 10 or 11 year olds upwards – Any number – Indoors – Equip-
ment: pictures of well-known personalities.*
Before the party, cut out pictures of prominent personalities from
newspapers and magazines. Players have to guess the identities and
each player scores points for every correct guess. Part of the fun is in
choosing pictures of people in unusual settings.

123 GUESS THE BIRD

*For 11 year olds upwards – Any number – Indoors – Equipment:
paper, pencils.*

Players are provided with ten cryptic clues which contain the names
of ten well-known birds. The player with the most correct answers

wins a prize.

The ten clues (and answers) are:

1.	What's done with food after chewing.	SWALLOW
2.	A portion of the whole and a range of hills.	PART RIDGE
3.	A Monarch and a person who lives from the sea.	KING FISHER
4.	What a coward does in time of danger.	QUAIL
5.	Found in a pod and what you do with a snoot.	PEA COCK
6.	A childish prank.	LARK
7.	A famous architect.	WREN
8.	To lower the head from danger.	DUCK
9.	Whose eye is very sharp.	EAGLE
10.	Something bright in the sky at night and a moorland plant.	STAR LING

124 KNOW YOUR PARTNER

Icebreaker – Any age over 10 or 11 – Equal numbers of girls and boys – Indoors – Equipment: none.

Each of the male players is told to choose a partner of the opposite sex. He must stare intently at his chosen partner for exactly one minute. Then the girls are sent out of the room and each player in turn is asked to describe the person he has just looked at – giving colour of eyes, colour of hair, shape of nose, pattern and colour of dress, etc. The most correct description wins.

125 GEOGRAPHY

Icebreaker – Any age over 9 or 10 – Any number – Indoors – Equipment: a matchbox.

Players sit in a circle and a matchbox is given to the first player. He calls out the name of a city somewhere in the United States, and throws the box to any other player. The person catching the box must give the state in which the town is placed. If he fails to give an answer in ten seconds, he loses a point. He can challenge the first player if he chooses, but if the right answer is given, he loses another point. The game continues as each player challenges others to place the town. When a player has lost ten points he drops out of the game.

126 SLIPPER TAP

Any age over 6 – Any number – Indoors – Equipment: a slipper or rolled newspaper.

Players form a circle standing shoulder to shoulder, and an odd man out is chosen to stand blindfolded in the centre of the circle. Then the players pass a slipper or a rolled-up newspaper behind their backs and any player can at any time tap the odd man out lightly on the legs or shoulders with the slipper. As soon as he is tapped the odd man out makes a grab for the person he thinks has tapped him. As soon as he touches someone, all players must freeze. If the odd man out has picked out the player holding the slipper, then the two exchange places. If he has picked out the wrong person, however, the game continues.

127 ORANGE CHIN CHIN RELAY

Teenagers or adults – Any number, in 2 teams – Indoors or outdoors – Equipment: 2 oranges.

Divide the players into two teams, and stand each team in a line. Each team leader then tucks an orange under his chin. On the word 'GO' he must turn around and transfer the orange to the next team member without using his hands. The winning team will be the one which has successfully transferred the orange right down the line without dropping it. If it drops, the team must start again. See drawing.

128 POTATO JOUSTING

For boys over 9 or 10. This is a rough-and-tumble game for strong children – Even numbers – Indoors or outdoors – Equipment: 2 table-spoons and 1 potato for half the number of players.

The players sort themselves into two teams, and each team chooses its horses and knights. Knights are armed with two tablespoons and a small potato. They place the potato in one spoon and use the other spoon as a 'sword'.

'Horses' go down on their hands and knees and their knights ride on their backs. The object of the contest is to knock your opponent's potato out of his spoon without losing your own.

If you like, you can play this as a knockout game until there is one pair of overall winners. A prize may then be given.

129 CRISP WHISTLE

Icebreaker – Adults – Any even number – Indoors – Equipment: a package of potato chips for each player.

This little game is always good for a laugh — particularly if there are a few people who can't whistle very well. Two teams line up and each player is given a handful of chips. Then, given a starting signal, the first member of each team eats his chips as quickly as possible, and then whistles the chorus from 'Yankee Doodle' (or any other short tune that everyone knows). As soon as one person has finished whistling, the next team member eats his chips and whistles. The first team to finish is the winner.

130 SNOWY MOUNTAIN

Any age over 8 or 9 — Any number — Indoors — Equipment: a deep pie pan, a plate, a bag of flour, a chocolate drop, a table knife.

Fill the pie pan with flour, hold the plate over the top of the pan, and turn plate and pan upside down together. Carefully remove the pan, so that you are left with a moulded dome of flour on the plate. Gently place the chocolate drop on top of this, in the very centre, and you are then ready to begin the game. Using the table knife, each player in turn must slice away a portion of the flour. The object is to keep the chocolate drop on top of the snowy mountain for as long as possible, so it pays each player to cut the very smallest slice that he can. The hapless player who finally causes the mountain to collapse and the chocolate drop to fall has to place both hands behind his back, bend over the plate, pick the chocolate up with his teeth and then eat it. Rather messy, but fun!

131 CAT AND RAT

Any age over 5 or 6 — From 10 to 20 players — Indoors or outdoors — Equipment: none.

Another boisterous game this — for any number of players between ten and twenty. Players hold hands and form a circle. Two other players are chosen to be Cat and Rat. Rat stands inside the circle, and Cat stands outside. The object of the game is for Cat to catch Rat ... but the players in the circle must do everything they can to stop Cat getting through into the middle of the circle. Cat can try to crawl under legs, push through the circle of locked arms or even to barge his way through. When he eventually succeeds in breaking through the circle and catching his Rat, the two players from the point in the circle where he broke through become the next Cat and Rat.

132 BOMB AIMERS

Any age over 7 or 8 – Any even number – Indoors – Equipment: 2 or 3 dining chairs, darts and a dartboard.

Put two or three dining chairs side by side. This is the bomb-aimers' bay. A dartboard is put flat on the floor beside the last chair. Players lie on their stomachs on the chairs and have to drop (no throwing) their bomb darts on to the target. Double 20 being furthest away counts as enemy ammunition depot (10 points), treble 20 counts as enemy airfield (5 points), bullseye counts as enemy searchlight (1 point). Teams take turns with three 'bombs' for each player. Arm must be straight at moment of 'bombs away' and chins may be no further out than the edge of the chair seat.

133 AROUND THE WORLD

Any age – Any number – Indoors – Equipment: a chair for each player except one.

You need a chair for each player in this game except one. Arrange them in a circle, facing inwards. Every player takes a seat and is given a piece of paper bearing the name of a city – and the extra player stands in the middle. He then calls out that he is making a journey from one city to another. For instance, he might say: 'I am going from London to Paris'. As he speaks, the players who represent the cities mentioned must exchange seats quickly. The player in the middle must try to occupy one of the empty seats first – and if he does, the player left standing takes his place in the middle. From time to time, the player in the middle can also call out that he is 'Taking a trip around the world' . . . when ALL seated players must get up and change seats. The trick of the game is for the player in the middle to remember which of the other players have which city names.

134 OCEAN WAVE

Any age – Any number – Indoors – Equipment: a chair for every player except one.

When people have tired of playing 'Around the World', the chairs are perfectly laid out for yet another popular circle game. Once again, every player but one sits down and one person is left standing in the middle. He calls out either 'Shift Right' or 'Shift Left'. When it is 'Shift Right' every player moves two chairs to the right. When 'Shift Left' each player moves two places to the left. The leader can call several 'Lefts' in a row and then add to the confusion by suddenly changing back to a 'Shift Right' command. This is when he will have the best chance of grabbing a spare seat for himself and putting the unlucky player without a chair in the middle.

135 COP AND ROBBER

Any age over 7 or 8 – Any even number – Indoors or outdoors – Equipment: none.

Choose two players as the Cop and the Robber. All the rest form lines and hold hands. In between the lines of players are streets and alleyways. The cop must catch the robber, who runs in and out of the streets – but neither of them can pass through players with their hands linked. As the chase goes on, a leader can call out 'Change' at any minute. Then the players drop hands, make a quarter turn and link up again. So the street is no longer clear, but blocked at both ends, and runs in the opposite direction. Cop and Robber must now quickly change their tactics

136 FIND THE RATTLE

Any age over 6 or 7 — Any number — Indoors or outdoors — Equipment: a tin box containing paper clips or buttons, blindfold.

For this game you will need a small tin box, containing a few buttons or paper clips to make the box rattle. Then one player is chosen to be 'it' and stands in the middle of the circle formed by all the other players. He is blindfolded and pointed towards the person holding the rattle. The rattle is then thrown (not passed) to any other player. As soon as the player catches it, he must shake it quickly to make a noise and then throw it quickly to someone else. 'It' has to point out the person holding the rattle. When he does so, he joins the circle and the caught player becomes 'It.'

137 SNAKE BY THE TAIL

Any age over 5 or 6 — Any number — Outdoors if possible — Equipment: none.

This game is best played outdoors, but if you have plenty of room, it can be played indoors. Players line up behind one another and grasp the waist of the person in front. The object of the game is for the person at the front end of the 'snake' to touch the person at the tail. To do this, the leader has to drag everyone else with him, and anyone who lets go and breaks the 'snake' is out of the game. When the first player manages to touch the tail, he or she goes to the back of the line and the next person becomes the 'snake's' head.

138 POSTURE

Any age over 4 – Any number – Indoors – Equipment: music, and one book for each child.

The players have to walk round the room to music with a book balanced on their heads. When the music stops, each player must stop, go down on one knee and raise both arms in the air WITHOUT dropping his book. Anyone who does goes out of the game and the music starts again. The game continues – and the last remaining player becomes the winner. See drawing.

139 SQUEAK PIGGY SQUEAK

Any age – Any number – Indoors or outdoors – Equipment: cushion and blindfold.

All players sit in a circle and one player is chosen to be blindfolded. He is given a cushion which he places on someone's lap and then sits on it. The blindfolded player then says: 'Squeak, Piggy, Squeak' and the person he is sitting on must squeak three times. The blindfolded player must then guess who he is sitting on. If he guesses right, he joins the circle and 'piggy' becomes the next player in the blindfold.

140 BALLOON BASKETBALL

Any age over 10 or 11 – 2 teams of 5 to 10 players – Large room – Equipment: 2 chairs and 2 balloons for each round.

You need plenty of room for this game . . . and it can become a little boisterous, so keep it in a room which is fairly clear.

Two teams of between five and ten players are chosen. The pitch is marked out by two chairs at opposite ends of the room. Each team chooses one player to stand on one of the chairs.

Each team is then given a balloon and the object of the game is to get the opposing team's balloon to the man on the chair so that he can burst it. Balloons must be kept in the air at all times, either by hitting or blowing, and no-one is allowed to hold on to a balloon or to pass it to another player. The players on the chairs are not allowed to move off them. The game gets quite hectic when each player is trying to protect his own team's balloon and destroy that of his opponents at the same time.

141 FUNNY HEADLINES

Any age over 10 or 11 – Any even number – Indoors – Equipment: newspapers, scissors, paper and paste or adhesive tape.

Each team is handed a few pages from any popular newspaper. With scissors and paste, using only complete words taken from headlines or display advertisements, funny headlines of at least four words have to be concocted against a deadline of, say, five minutes. The greatest number of funny new headlines wins. Each word over six in a new headline scores an extra point.

Every word must be cut from the paper as it appears – individual letters are barred, only complete words allowed. The pasted-down headlines may, of course, be of all mixed sizes and type faces.

142 TRAVELS

Any age over 7 or 8 – Any number – Indoors – Equipment: none.

Any number of people can play this game. The first player starts out by announcing that he is going to travel to some country or town. He might announce that he is going to Birmingham. The next player must quickly say the name of a country or town which begins with the last letter in the previous player's place name. For instance, he might announce that he is going to Manchester. The next player must then think of a place starting with the letter R and so on until everyone has had a go.

143 TRAVELLING WORKERS

Any age over 10 or 11 – Any number – Indoors – Equipment: none.

This game is a much more complicated variation of the one above. Very young children would find it too difficult, so it's definitely for the older ones. The first player says that he is going to a certain place and also what he is going to do for work when he gets there. It becomes more complicated when you realise that the job has to start with the same letter as the place.

For instance, if our player from the 'Travels' game said he was going to Birmingham ... in THIS game he might say something like : 'I am going to Birmingham where I shall bake better biscuits'. The next player could go to Manchester and make modern matchsticks, and so on.

144 MUSICAL PARCEL

Any age over 4 – Any number – Indoors or outdoors – Equipment: small prize in many wrappings, and music.

Before the party, choose a small prize – such as a bar of chocolate, or a small toy – and wrap it in many different layers of paper. The parcel is passed round from child to child while music is playing. Each time the music stops, whoever is holding the parcel takes off one of the layers of wrapping paper. The lucky player who takes off the last wrapping keeps the prize.

145 INITIAL I-SPY

Icebreaker – Any age – Any number – Indoors – Equipment: none.

This variation on the old I-spy game is very useful as a party opener, because it gives everyone a chance to be introduced to everyone else. Each person starts out by telling everyone else his name. Then he looks around the room and in one minute names all the objects in the room that begin with his initials. So if Sammy Jones stands up, he might see a sofa, sausages, seats, scrapbook – and, perhaps, a jug, jar, jack-in-the-box. No prizes for the winner in this one . . . because obviously people with names like Zacharias or Zelda start off with a bit of a handicap

146 GHOSTS

Any age from 10 or 11 – Any number (the more the merrier) – Indoors – Equipment: none.

The more people playing this game the better. The first player calls out any letter of the alphabet, but he must have a word in mind when he says his letter. The letter should be the first letter of the word he has thought of. For instance, if he thinks of the word 'Clock', he calls out 'C'.

The next player must give the second letter, but he can think of any word he likes. He might, for instance, think of the word 'Crossword' . . . so that he will say 'CR'.

The next player might immediately think of the word 'Crocodile'

57

and call out 'CRO'. As you can see, the game becomes progressively more difficult as it goes on. The player who makes a complete word by adding the last letter gets a point against him and becomes one-third of a ghost. Also any player who fails to call out a new letter quickly becomes one-third of a ghost. Any player may challenge another at any time by asking what word he had in mind. If the challenged player is not able to give a sensible answer, then he too becomes a third of a ghost. Three failures make a player a full ghost and he fades out of the game.

147 THE DONKEY'S TAIL

Any age over 5 or 6 – Any number – Indoors – Equipment: drawing of a donkey, blindfold, and a pen or pencil.

Pin a picture of a donkey on the wall and line up the contestants, Blindfold the first person in the line and give him a pen or pencil. Tell him to draw in the donkey's tail – and ask all the other competitors in turn to do the same. The one who places the tail nearest to the donkey is the winner. See drawing.

148 RING A RING O' ROSES

Small children – Any number – Indoors or outdoors – Equipment: none.

All players form a circle, holding hands and dance round singing the famous old song:

'Ring-a-ring o' roses
A pocket full of posies.
A-tishoo !, A-tishoo !
We all fall down.'

Upon the word 'down' all players must fall to the floor. The last one down is out each time.

149 CREEPING JENNY

Small children – Any odd number – Indoors or outdoors – Equipment: none.

One player stands at the end of the room with his back to the others. The other players are divided into pairs. Hand in hand, they try to creep up quietly to touch 'Jenny' – who turns round if he hears a sound and sends the pair back to the start. The first pair to touch 'Jenny' are the winners.

150 SPARROWS AND STATUES

Small children – Any number – Indoors or outdoors – Equipment: none.

All players pretend to be sparrows, flying and hopping about and flapping their arms. The game leader calls 'stop' at any time and then everyone must freeze like a statue. Anyone who moves is out of the game. A small prize could be given for the funniest pose.

151 REVERSE RACE

Any age over 7 or 8 – Even numbers – Outdoors – Equipment: none.

Form a group of boys and girls, pair them off facing one another, and holding hands. Then line them up with the boys' backs to the finishing line. For the first race, the boy (running backwards) pulls the girl. Then they change over and the girl pulls the boy. First home are the winners, unless of course, you caught them cheating by looking round !

152 LEAPFROG RELAY

Boys over 9 or 10 – Any even number – Outdoors – Equipment: none.

Form two teams and line them up in two rows. One man out in front of each team then bends over forming a 'back'. The other members of the team stand with their legs far apart with the exception of the last man. On the word 'GO' he must crawl through the tunnel of his team's legs, leapfrog the man at the front and then take over from him. The person who was 'leapfrogged' then joins the front of his team and the new 'back man' crawls through the tunnel of legs and leapfrogs the new front man. And so on.

153 PANDORA'S BOX

Any age over 8 or 9 — Any number — Indoors — Equipment: 3 small objects per child, wrapping paper, large box.

Take a series of three objects, wrap them up together, and place them in a large cardboard box. Ask the first competitor to take a parcel from the box, untie it and look at his three articles. Then ask him to tell a story for two minutes involving all the three articles. The best story wins a prize.

154 THE GREAT CHEESE TEST

Adults — Any number — Indoors — Equipment: small pieces of different cheeses, cheesecloth, pencils and paper.

Small pieces of many kinds of cheeses in tiny quantities are wrapped up, preferably in cheesecloth, and a number tag added. The names of the cheeses — Danish blue, Blue Stilton and so on — are listed, and a copy of the list given to each player.

The players then have to identify which cheese is which on their list by smell alone. If you want to be really nasty you can wrap a piece of soap as well, give it an exotic name, and see who spots it.

155 ANIMAL FARM

Any age over 5 or 6 — Any number — Indoors or outdoors — Equipment: a pencil and paper for each player.

Whisper to each player the name of an animal. On the word 'GO' each player makes the appropriate noise of that animal. Set a time limit of say two minutes, and at the end let each player write down the different animal noises that were made. The person with the most correct names wins.

156 ASSOCIATIONS

Any age over 8 or 9 — Any number — Indoors — Equipment: none.

Form a circle of chairs with the children comfortably seated. Call on one player to think of a word, and the person on his right must then say a word associated with the previous one. Anyone who pauses drops out, and the last person in is the winner. Example: SHIP — boat, battleship, cruiser, paddle, oar, canoe, sea, water, ocean, river, lake, etc.

157 STORY GAME

Any age over 7 or 8 — Any number divisible by 3 — Indoors — Equipment: none.

Seat the children in groups of three. Then ask one child to start to tell

a story. At the end of a minute the next child in the group should continue the story and the third child bring it to a logical conclusion. Ask each group in turn for a story. If you wish you can run this on a competitive basis, so that each time a child gets lost, he drops out. This is a good game for giving children experience in speaking.

158 HULLABALLOO

Any age over 5 — Any even number — Indoors — Equipment: beans or similar small objects.

Scatter around the room a number of beans or similar small objects. Divide the players into teams of four or five, one of whom is the leader. When the other members of the team find one of the objects they must make the noise of an animal (pre-arranged with the leader) until the leader collects the object. The team whose leader collects the most objects is the winner. See drawing.

159 MUSICAL CANDIES

Small children — Any number — Indoors — Equipment: a wrapped candy for each child, and music.

A nice variation on the ever-popular game of Musical Chairs. Arrange chairs in a circle — one chair for each child — hand each child a wrapped candy and parade them around the circle in time to music. When the music is stopped each child must dash and put his candy on a vacant chair. Of course, this is too easy, so the second time you start the music remove one of the chairs . . . one child will be left out when the music stops. Continue to remove the chairs until there is only one successful child left with a candy on the last chair.

160 KNOCKOUT

Any age over 6 or 7 — Any number — Indoors or outdoors — Equipment: 1 soft ball.

Stand the players in a circle and let them throw a soft ball to each other, catching it with two hands. If a player drops a ball he must then pay a penalty:

First time — Kneels on one knee but uses both hands.
Second time — Kneels on both knees but uses both hands.
Third time — Kneels on both knees and uses right hand.
Fourth time — Kneels on both knees and uses left hand.
Fifth time — He is out.

Each time a player catches a ball while paying a penalty he regains one place. It sometimes takes hours to find the eventual winner — so here's hoping the children tire before you do.

161 KNIGHTS ON HORSEBACK

A boys' game for any age over 10 or 11 — Any even number — Outdoors — Equipment: none.

This is a rough and tumble game but very popular among young boys. Pair off the boys and get one to give his friend a 'piggyback'. In other words one partner is the horse, the other the knight. Two pairs then meet in 'combat' and the winners are the pair who force the opposition to fall or dismount. The winners then go on to take on the next challenging pair. Best played on grass.

162 KING OF THE CASTLE

Any age over 5 or 6 — Any number — Indoors — Equipment: 1 newspaper.

Place a newspaper on the floor and let one of the players stand on it declaring that he is King Of The Castle. It is then up to another player to pull him off the newspaper. The successful one then takes over as 'King Of The Castle'. See drawing.

163 JAPANESE TAG

Any age over 5 or 6 — Any number — Outdoors — Equipment: none.

The odd man out in this case is not the most popular of people and the others do not want to get near him. When he touches someone the person touched must hold himself in the spot where he was touched. Then the person touched joins ranks with the odd man out and tries to touch another child. In the end you are faced with children in all sorts of positions. The last person to get caught is the winner.

164 FUNNY-GRAMS

Any age over 7–8 – Any number – Indoors – Equipment: pencil and paper for each player.

A leader is chosen and all other players are given a sheet of paper and a pencil. Then the leader calls out four letters of the alphabet. Each player must make up a sentence using words beginning with the four letters in order.

For instance, suppose the leader called out 'A B I H' – a possible sentence could be : 'A Bear Is Hairy'.

When everyone has written a sentence, they take it in turns to read it out loud. This is where the fun begins, and anyone who cannot make up a sentence pays a forfeit.

All players take a turn to be the leader.

165 VOCABULARY SPEED

Any age over 7 or 8 – Any number – Indoors – Equipment: pencil and paper for each player. The timekeeper will need a clock or watch.

Each player is given a pencil and paper. The timekeeper sets a time limit – say, fifteen seconds – and calls out a letter of the alphabet. The players then write down as many words as they can which begin with that letter. When the allotted time is up, the timekeeper calls another letter. After four letters the total number of words for each player is added up and the one with the most wins.

166 MEMORY TEST (KIM'S GAME)

Any age over 6 or 7 – Any number – Indoors – Equipment: a variety of objects, a tray, pencils and paper.

Collect a variety of objects on a tray, place the tray on a table and let the players look at it for thirty seconds. Then remove the tray, give the players pencils and paper and ask them to list the objects on the tray. The person with the most correct answers is the winner.

167 TEAKETTLE

Any age over 7–8 – Any number – Indoors – Equipment: none.

One of the players leaves the room and the rest of the group decide upon a certain word and three sentences in which the word could be used. To make this game more fun, it is best to choose words which have several different meanings, uses or spellings.

Suppose the chosen word were 'TIDE'. This could be used as 'Tied'; 'BLEW' could be 'Blue' and so on.

To use the first example – the word 'TIDE'. The three sentences might be as follows:

'The (TEAKETTLE) came in quickly.'
'The two runners (TEAKETTLE) for first place.'
'The ropes were (TEAKETTLE) together.'
. . . That's the catch, you see. When the players say the sentences, they don't use the chosen word at all, but say 'Teakettle' instead. The unlucky player who is outside the room has to come in and guess what the word is. Players take turns to go outside.

168 MAD HATTER

Any age over 5 or 6 – Any number – Outdoors – Equipment: 1 old hat.

For this chasing game you need an old hat. One player is chosen to be 'It' and the others pass the hat round from one to another. No player may refuse to accept the hat, and he must wear it until he has caught someone else to pass it on to. While all this is going on, 'It' is trying to catch a person actually wearing the hat. If 'It' does so, then they exchange places. The game gets fast and furious as players rush around trying to catch another victim to wear the hat, and 'It' chases around trying to be in the right place at the right time.

169 UP JENKINS

Any age over 5 – Any even number – Indoors – Equipment: a penny.

Two teams are seated on opposite sides of a table. Toss up to see which team has first go and give the winners a penny. That team must pass the penny up and down the line *underneath* the table. The opposite team's captain then shouts: 'UP JENKINS' and the 'Coin Holding' team place their hands on the table – fists clenched. The opposition have two goes, for a point, at finding which player is holding the penny. The opposition captain points to a clenched hand and says: 'THIS HAND', and if the coin is not in that hand he can choose another, saying: 'THAT HAND'. If successful, he scores a point for his team. After each two guesses, the penny is passed to the opposing team. Ten points will constitute a game.

170 TAP TAP

Any age over 5 or 6 – Any number – Indoors – Equipment: a pencil.

All players move to one end of the room and turn their backs on the leader. The leader, with a pencil, taps any object in the room that makes a noise. The players, without turning round, have to guess what the leader is tapping with his pencil. The first player to guess correctly becomes the next leader.

171 WHAT'S THE TIME MR. WOLF?

Any age over 5 – Any number – Outdoors – Equipment: none.

This is a variation of 'He'. One player is chosen as Mr. Wolf, then he walks away to be followed by the others who ask: 'What's the time, Mr. Wolf?' He then replies with any time he likes: One, Two, Three o'clock, and so on. When Mr. Wolf replies: 'Twelve o'clock. Dinner time', the followers have to run for home before being caught. The last one home, or the one caught, is the next Mr. Wolf.

172 CHARADES

Any age from 6 or 7 to 70 – Teams of 4 – Indoors – Equipment: old clothes for the actors.

Dressing up adds to the fun of this game. Divide the players into teams of about four. Draw lots to see who will act first and send the winners out of the room. The players must choose a word of two or three syllables. Each syllable must be acted in a separate scene and then finally the whole word. For example: 'Ear', then 'Wig', and finally 'Earwig'. The other teams must try to guess the chosen word. The team that guesses has the next turn.

173 MIME GAME

Any age from 5 or 6 – Any even number – Indoors – Equipment: none.

The players are divided into teams and each team in turn acts a saying or Nursery Rhyme. This must be done in mime otherwise you will give the game away too quickly. The other teams must guess which saying or Nursery Rhyme is being acted. The team that guesses gets the next turn.

174 THE SCENT GAME

Any age over 6 or 7 – Any number – Indoors – Equipment: empty jars containing 'smelly' foods, a pencil and paper each.

Place a variety of foods in some empty jars and call in your blindfolded contestants. When all have sniffed the various jars give them all a pencil and paper to write down the different foods. e.g. onion, pineapple, smoked bacon, tea, coffee, cocoa, orange, lemon, cheese, cloves, etc.

175 SCANDAL

Any age over 6 or 7 – Any number – Indoors – Equipment: none.

The players sit in a long line or a circle. The first, turning to the second, whispers very rapidly some remark or brief sentence. The second, who may hear it distinctly, but probably doesn't, then whispers it as exactly as he can to the third player – and so on until

the line or circle is finished. The last player then whispers it to the first player, who repeats out loud his original remark, followed by the version of it which has just reached him. The difference between the two is often hilarious!

176 TIDDLYWINKS

Any age over 6 or 7 – Any number – Indoors – Equipment: a few dozen flat buttons, both large and small, and some eggcups.

Take a few dozen buttons and some eggcups, and tell the children to flip the buttons into the eggcups. The easiest way is to place the eggcups in a row, put the smaller buttons on the floor opposite each cup, and flip them in by pressing the back of the small button with the front of a larger button. The person who gets his buttons into the eggcup in the smallest number of 'flips' is the winner. See drawing.

177 CHAIN GAME

Any age over 4 – Any number – Outdoors – Equipment: none.

For this game you need a fairly large lawn or garden. One person is chosen as odd man out, and the other players scatter around the area. The odd man out must chase the others, and everyone caught links arms. The other players try to escape from the ever-building 'chain', but it will become increasingly difficult. The last person caught is the winner.

178 SCAVENGER HUNT

Any age over 5 or 6 – Any number – Indoors or outdoors – Equipment: list of various household or garden objects (small enough to be carried).

Prepare lists of objects from either inside or outside the house and issue these to the competitors. Set a one-minute time limit, and on the word 'GO' the players set off to collect the items listed. After the minute is up, the player with the greatest number of articles is the winner.

179 BOXES

Any age over 7 or 8 – Any smallish number – Indoors – Equipment: paper and pencils.

You need a sheet of paper and a pencil for each player. Draw seven lines of seven dots, one under the other. The object is to draw boxes. The first player draws a line connecting any two dots; the second player does likewise. Each player takes his turn to join up the dots, being careful not to link the third side of any square if he can help it, as this will give the next player the chance of completing a box. When he does this, he puts his initials in the box, and has another turn, possibly completing several boxes in one go. The player with the most boxes wins.

180 SHADOWS

Any age over 5 or 6 — 2 teams of any number — Indoors — Equipment: a sheet and a strong lamp.

Hang a sheet across the room in front of a strong lamp. Turn off all other lights. Divide the players into two teams. Each team passes behind the sheet, one at a time, disguising their appearance as much as they can, by wobbling, wiggling and so on — while the second team must guess who the shadow belongs to. The light is only turned on when the person is behind the sheet.

181 PIGGY-IN-THE-MIDDLE

Any age over 5 or 6 — 3 players — Outdoors — Equipment: 1 ball.

You need three players and a ball. Two players stand as far apart as they wish and the third one in the middle. The two outside players throw the ball to each other while the 'piggy in the middle' tries to catch it. As soon as he does, he changes places with whoever threw the ball, and he then becomes the 'piggy in the middle'.

182 BEETLE

Any age over 5 — Any number — Indoors — Equipment: 1 die, plus pencil and paper for each player.

You need one die, and paper and pencil for each player. Each player throws the die and each must throw a 'six' before starting the game. Then each player again throws the die, and draws the part of a beetle which his die number allows. Go on throwing until one player has drawn a whole beetle. He is the winner.
Rules
Throw a 6 to start the game. Then: 6 — Body; 5 — Head; 4 — Arms and legs; 3 — Feet and hands; 2 — Eyes; 1 — Nose and mouth.

183 I SPY

Any age over 5 — Any number — Indoors or outdoors — Equipment: none.

This old favourite is started off by one player saying: 'I spy with my little eye something beginning with...' The player finishes by saying a letter and the other players have to guess what the word is. The first to guess correctly chooses the next object.

184 FOX AND RABBITS

Any age from 4 — Any even number — Indoors — Equipment: chalk to draw lines and circles.

At each end of a large clear room draw lines representing home and sanctuary. In between draw a few small circles to represent rabbit holes. Divide the players into two teams — 'rabbits' and 'foxes'. The 'rabbits' dash from home to the sanctuary, the 'foxes' try to tag them, and anyone tagged drops out. The 'rabbits' may pop into a hole for a rest, but in the end when all the 'rabbits' are tagged or safe in the sanctuary, the teams change rôles and the team with the fewest eliminated wins.

185 FRENCH HE

Any age over 4 — Any number — Outdoors — Equipment: none.

The player chosen to be 'He' must catch one of the other players by touching him on some part of the body. The player caught must then put his hand on the part touched and keep it there until he has managed to touch another player. If touched on the foot a player must hop after the others.

186 STRAW RACE

Any age over 8 or 9 — about 6 players at a time — Indoors — Equipment: 20 small paper squares, a pencil, a large salad bowl, some straws.

Cut up 20 small squares of paper, mark an X on 3 of them, and put all the pieces in an empty salad bowl. Each player is given a straw and, on the word 'GO', has to try to pick up one of the squares marked X by sucking through his straw. The fun begins when two or more players are trying to pick up the same square. Each player must then suck as hard as he can in order to beat the others. Tapping the paper square to take it from another player is not allowed. The first person to lift an X square clear of the bowl is the winner. Unmarked squares do not count.

187 WOOLLY WILLIE

Any age — Any even number — Indoors — Equipment: dice, one cardigan sweater.

A sweater, preferably with a lot of buttons, is put on Woolly Willie. When dice are thrown by two teams in turn, the winner acts. The Decency League do up one button. The Immodests undo one. The aim is either to have the cardigan totally undone in 12 throws or totally done up. The Decency league are at an advantage since the cardigan starts off done up. Twelve throws (a number decided by the number of buttons) constitutes a round. Decide beforehand how many rounds you want to play and count to see whether more are done up or undone to decide the winner.

188 LEAPFROG

For children of 7 to 10 – Any number – Outdoors – Equipment: none.

This game should be played out of doors on soft ground. The first player makes a 'back' by bending well forward, his hands on his knees and his head tucked in. Another player then runs towards him, places his hands on his back and, with his legs wide apart, leaps over him. He runs a few yards further and bends over to make another 'back'. Any number of players can join in, each making a 'back' after he has jumped over all the others. Anyone who does not jump right over is out after 3 attempts.

189 JACK-IN-THE-BOX TAG

Any age from 4 – Any odd number – Indoors – Equipment: none.

Seat all the players except for one in two rows and let odd man out patrol down the aisle. On the word 'GO' the seated 'jacks' start bobbing up and down and the odd man must tage them while they are up. Those tagged stay sitting until there is an eventual winner.

190 KING CAESAR

Any age from 5 or 6 – Any number – Indoors or outdoors – Equipment: none except marked divisions.

For this game of tag the room or lawn is divided into three sections, the central one narrow and containing two catchers. The other players try to run through without being caught. If caught, they drop out, until you are left with one winner.

191 SPIN THE PLATE

Any age over 5 – Any number – Indoors – Equipment: an old enamel plate.

For this game you will need an old enamel plate. Players sit on the floor in a circle and 'It' stands in the centre. 'It' spins the plate, calls out someone's name and runs for his place in the circle. The person named must rush and catch the plate before it stops spinning and/or before 'It' has taken his place.

192 TOSS THE BOX

Any age over 5-6 — Any number — Indoors — Equipment: some paper plates, empty matchboxes, string or adhesive tape for starting line, a clock or wristwatch.

Mark out a starting line across the floor with string or adhesive tape. Place the paper plates about four feet beyond this, and hand the players an equal number of matchboxes each. Kneeling down behind the starting line, the players have to toss the matchboxes onto the plates. The player who scores highest within an allotted time (say, three minutes) is the winner.

193 SWEET-BAG TOUCH

Any age over 5 — Any number — Outdoors — Equipment: a small strong bag of wrapped candy.

Players form a circle leaving one person as odd man out, and he stands in the centre of the circle holding the bag of candy. The odd man out then tosses the bag to someone in the circle and runs out of the circle. The receiver catches the bag, places it back in the circle and chases the odd man out, who tries to pop back into the circle and touch the candy bag before he's 'tagged'. If he fails, he's out. If he succeeds, then he joins the circle and the receiver becomes odd man out. At a given moment of time the holder of the candy wins — and keeps them.

194 HIT TAG

Any age over 5 or 6 — Any number — Outdoors — Equipment: 1 soft ball.

Take the players out on the lawn and give the odd man out a small soft ball. On the word 'GO' the odd man out throws the ball about and the others must try to avoid being hit by it. He must not throw the ball too hard or any higher than knee height. When a player is hit he must drop out. The last person left in is the winner.

195 PUSSY IN THE CORNER

Any age over 4 — 5 players at a time — Indoors — Equipment: none.

Select five players, and stand one player in each corner of a room and one in the centre — the odd man out. On the word 'GO', the players in the four corners must dash clockwise and try to make the next corner before odd man out reaches one. If the odd man out is successful, then the person left out becomes odd man out. Or you can make a slight variation and invite the next player to come in and join the game.

196 SHELL GATHERERS

Any age over 5 or 6 — Any even number — Outdoors — Equipment: a variety of odds and ends.

Indicate a dividing line halfway across a lawn and form the players into two teams. One group will be the waves, the others the shell gatherers. On the gatherers' side of the line place a variety of odds and ends that the gatherers must pick up and take to 'home' (a predetermined place). While doing so the waves will come running out and try to tag the gatherers before they can reach 'home'. When all the gatherers have been caught the teams change places.

197 STRETCH TAG

Any age over 5 – 2 players at a time – Indoors or outdoors – Equipment: none.

This is a game for two players, and can be played on a knockout basis. The players stand face to face just a little more than arms' length apart and with their feet wide apart. Each player then tries to touch his opposite number without being touched. The winner will then take on the next challenger.

198 STATUE TAG

Any age over 5 – Any number – Indoors or outdoors – Equipment: none.

Choose one person as 'IT', and divide the rest of the players into two sections. Some will be statues and stand completely still; the others will be runners. On the word 'GO' the runners dash round and 'IT' will try to tag them before they can achieve safety by holding the hand of one of the statues. The statues become the runners next time.

199 SILLY SPEECHES

For teenagers or adults — Any number up to 10 — Indoors — Equipment: none, but the judge will need a clock or wristwatch.

First, ask competitors to remove all wristwatches, and cover up any clocks. Each player then has to make a speech on any subject of his choice for a given time which has been specified by the judge (say, thirty seconds or a minute). The important thing is that the player must judge for himself when the time limit is reached, and then stop talking. The judge notes the time taken by each player, and the one whose speech has run nearest to the allotted time is the winner.

200 SEW THE BUTTONS RACE

Any age over 9 or 10 – Team game – Indoors – Equipment: a piece of cloth, a needle and a reel of cotton for each team, a shirt button for each team member.

Give each team member a button, and put the needles, cotton and pieces of cloth on a table. At the word 'GO' the first member of each team runs to the table, sews a button on to the cloth, then runs back, so that the next person can start. The first team to sew all their buttons on their piece of cloth wins.

201 PENNY WINNING

Any age over 5 or 6 — Any number — Indoors — Equipment: a checkered cloth or piece of linoleum, a handful of pennies.

Place a checkered cloth or piece of linoleum on a table, and arm the players with pennies. Stand them about three feet away and ask them to throw the pennies on to the table. The players keep any pennies which land in a square without touching the edges of the square — plus an extra penny for each successful throw.

202 OVER AND UNDER RELAY

For boys over 7 or 8 — Any even number — Outdoors — Equipment: none.

Form two teams and stand them in a line, a little apart. The rear man in each team leapfrogs the next man, crawls under the next one's legs, and so on down the line. When he reaches the front, he runs back to his original place, touches the next man on the shoulder, and off *he* goes. And so on till everyone has taken part. The first team home are the winners.

203 BALL WHEELBARROW RACE

For boys over 11 or 12 — Any number in pairs — Indoors or outdoors — Equipment: 1 ball for each pair.

Players choose partners and one of the pair goes down on his hands and knees. On the word 'GO' the partner picks him up by the knees and the 'barrow' places a ball in his hands and moves by rolling the ball. When they reach the finishing line they change places and return in the same way. First team home wins.

204 HOT POTATO

Any age over 5–6 – Any number – Indoors – Equipment: a small potato (or ball), a blindfold.

All the players should sit in a circle except one, who is blindfolded. The players pass a small potato (or a ball) to each other. They may pass it or throw it to anyone. Whoever is offered the potato must accept it and pass it on as quickly as possible. The blindfolded player calls out 'Hot Potato' at any time. When he calls, whoever is holding the potato has to stand up and pay a forfeit before leaving the game. The last player is the winner.

205 VARIATIONS

Any age over 7 or 8 – Any number – Indoors – Equipment: none.

Choose two teams and stand them in a line, facing each other. A leader is chosen to take charge of the action and act as judge, and he decides on the variations of posture to be allowed in the game. There can be any number of these – the more the merrier. For instance, the postures can be: sitting on the floor, kneeling, standing with hands in the air, bending down to touch toes, standing with hands on head, sitting with hands on head, etc. When the leader calls out 'MOVE' each player must adopt one of the postures agreed. The trick is to move into a posture quickly, but it must not be the same as that of the opposite member of the other team. If this happens, both players are out of the game and have to perform a forfeit.

206 SPEECHES

Icebreaker – Any age at all – Any number – Indoors – Equipment: none.

Before starting the game, write down an amusing, difficult or down-right ridiculous subject upon pieces of paper. Examples: 'Raising Kippers for Fun and Profit', 'My Adventures in The Steaming Jungles of Pongoland', 'The Fine Art of Scrimble-Scratching', 'A Thousand Uses for Second-hand Socks', 'Atomic Physics in The Year 2000', 'Party Political Speech on Behalf of The Pudding Party', 'How to Build Your Own Frankenstein Monster', 'A Concise History of Molasses Mining'.

Place the pieces of paper in a hat and invite each person to choose one, and then, in turn, stand up and deliver a two-minute speech on the subject he has picked. Any player who falters, stops or laughs at his own speech must pay a forfeit.

207 TABOO

Any age over 7–8 – Any number – Indoors – Equipment: none.

Everyone decides in advance that a certain letter of the alphabet is taboo. Then each player stands up and has to talk for one minute without using any words beginning with the forbidden letter. If they falter for too long, or use a word that starts with the forbidden letter, they must pay a forfeit.

208 HUNT THE THIMBLE

Any age over 4 – Any number – Indoors – Equipment: 1 thimble.

Send all the players out of the room, and hide the thimble somewhere within arm's reach. Then call the children back into the room to look for it. The successful finder then takes over as hider and the same game goes on as before.

209 LOOTING

Any age over 4 – Any even number – Indoors – Equipment: a pile of small articles.

Line two teams up at opposite ends of the room, and in the centre of the room place a number of odds and ends. On the word 'GO' all the players rush to the pile of oddments and take back one article at a time. When all the items have been collected the team with the most is declared the winner.

210 OFF THE DECK

Any age over 4 – Any number – Indoors – Equipment: a radio or record-player.

Players scatter around the room and hop, jump or skip to music. When the music stops the players must have one foot off the ground. Last off the ground is out; last person left in is the winner.

211 BOX TAG

Any age over 5 or 6 — Odd number — Indoors — Equipment: chalk or adhesive tape.

Place the children in four groups in four corners of the room and mark a square round each group with the chalk or tape. The odd man out is the key player who has to try to catch or tag the players as they dash from corner to corner. Anyone tagged drops out.

212 HOUSE OF CARDS

Any age over 6 or 7 – 2 teams of equal number – Indoors – Equipment: a pack of cards.

Each team is dealt twenty cards and has to build them into a card house. All the players take a turn, and one can support the house until it is complete. The first team with a house which can stand unsupported for five seconds with all the cards used is the winner.

213 GOAL TAG

Any age over 5 or 6 – Any number – Outdoors – Equipment: 2 plastic buckets.

Make a 'goal' about three yards wide with two plastic buckets, and choose an odd man out to stand in the goal. He has to stop the others from charging through the goal. Those he catches drop out.

214 SNAKE TAG

Any age over 5 or 6 – Any even number – Outdoors for preference – Equipment: none.

Form two teams of players into two lines, the player behind holding the waist of the person in front. On the word 'GO' the player in front of each team must try to catch the last person in the other team. When caught the tagged player drops out. The game continues until one team has only one player left. The other team thus wins.

215 TAIL TAG

Any age over 5 or 6 – Any number – Outdoors – Equipment: none.

Set all the players loose but three. They must try to tag the other players. When one player is caught he must join his 'tagger' and place his arms around the waist. Thus the team with the most members when all the players have been caught will be the winners.

216 WATCH TICK

Icebreaker – Any age over 8 or 9 – Any number – Indoors – Equipment: some envelopes, a pencil.

This game is terribly difficult and proves how little people know about their own possessions! Each player has to take off his watch, which is put into an envelope. After 'shuffling', the envelopes are numbered. The players then have to pick them up by a corner one by one and from the sound of the tick guess which watch is their own.

217 SPOOK

Any age over 8 or 9 – Any number – Indoors – Equipment: an old sheet.

One child plays the spook, with an old sheet over his head. Ask someone to stand by the light switch and turn the light off and on. All the players move around in the dark, and when the lights go on, everyone freezes. The spook then stands quite still and sees how many players he can touch with outstretched arms. These players, when touched, scream and go out of the game. This game can be repeated with a change of spook after a few players have been sent off.

218 SCRUM PUSH

Any age over 8 or 9 – Teams of up to 8 children – Outdoors (preferably on grass) – Equipment: a length of tape to mark the dividing line.

Mark a dividing line with the tape and form two teams of up to eight people per team. The teams must try to push each other completely over the line. The team that succeeds wins.

219 HOOP RELAY

Any age over 8 or 9 – 2 teams of up to 10 players – Outdoors – Equipment: a hoop for each team.

Form two teams of up to ten players and give the first person in each team a hoop. On the word 'GO' the first member drops the hoop over the head of the second person and lets it drop to the ground. He then picks it up and does the same to the next person, and so on until he reaches the end of the line. Then he returns to the front and the second person in the team takes over from him. The first team to complete the whole run are the winners. See drawing.

220 BALL ROLL RELAY

Any age over 6 or 7 – 2 teams of 6 – Outdoors – Equipment: 2 small balls.

Line up two teams of six children with their feet wide apart and give number one in the line a small ball. On the word 'GO' he must roll the ball through the legs of his team so that it reaches the child at the back. That player picks it up, runs to the front and again rolls the ball back through the team's legs. The game continues until the first man is back at the front. The first team to finish are the winners.

221 MATCHBOX TOWERS

Any age over 6–7 – Any number – Indoors – Equipment: 12 empty matchboxes.

The object of the game is to hold one hand in front of you, palm downwards, and see how many matchboxes you can pile on the back of your hand, one on top of the other. Each player takes it in turn to try, and the one who stacks up the biggest number of match-boxes is the winner.

222 PIRATE'S CHEST

Any age over 7 or 8 – Any number – Indoors or outdoors – Equipment: none.

In this alphabetical game, players have to think of words beginning with all the letters of the alphabet. Players sit around and chant:

Up in the attic is an old pirate's chest. In that chest there is an . . .

Each player in turn has to give a word using the letter 'A', then 'B' and so on. Letters like X and Z can be left out. Anyone who falters or gives a word beginning with the wrong letter is out.

223 WHAT'S MY LINE?

Any age over 8 or 9 – Teams of even numbers plus a referee – Indoors – Equipment: none.

Taken from the old TV series which was popular for years, this game is always good fun. Choose two teams, and have one player to act as referee. Each player in turn thinks up an unusual job or profession, and does a little mime as a starter clue. Then the challenging team has to guess the job by asking questions. If they guess the job in ten questions or less, they score a point. If they do not, the other team scores a point. Teams change round, and the one with the final highest score wins.

224 TIDDLYWINK GOLF

Any age over 8 or 9 – Any number – Indoors – Equipment: egg cups, books, rags and tiddlywinks (or buttons).

Using tiddlywink counters (or buttons), players battle their way round a miniature 'golf course' . . . with egg cups making the 'holes' and books and pieces of rags making 'bunkers' and 'sandtraps'. First player to complete the course wins.

225 SING ABOUT THE GIRLS

Teenagers – Any number – Indoors – Equipment: none.

Players take turns to sing a few lines from any popular song that has a girl's name in its title. Any player who cannot think of a song drops out of the game.

There are many songs with a girl's name in them . . . from 'Eleanor Rigby' or 'Peggy Sue' right down the line to 'Sweet Adeleine' or 'Oh! Susanna'.

226 SING ABOUT THE TOWNS

Teenagers – Any number – Indoors – Equipment: none.

This is a variation of the Sing About the Girls game, but instead of girls' names the songs must contain the name of a town in their titles.

For instance: 'San Francisco', 'By The Time I Get to Phoenix', 'London Bridge is Falling Down', 'Durham Town', etc.

227 SAUSAGES

Any age over 5 or 6 – Any number – Indoors – Equipment: none.

Players sit in a circle round the poor victim. They bombard him with questions, such as 'What is your favourite fruit?' 'How would you describe the shape of your nose?', etc. The victim has to answer 'sausages' to every question . . . and the first player to laugh or giggle is sent out of the game. If the victim laughs, he too is sent out, and a new victim chosen from the other players.

228 ROUND THE CLOCK

For teenagers or adults – Any number – Indoors – Equipment: a darts board and darts.

Players must get a double to start, then they each take turns to place a dart in the different segments, in numerical order. When a player reaches twenty, he must score another double and then a bullseye to win the game. See drawing.

229 SHANGHAI

For adults – Any number – Indoors – Equipment: a darts board and darts.

Each player throws three darts in turn, progressing exactly as in 'Round The Clock' – with the difference that he tries to score as many possible in each segment each time. If a player lands his three darts in the numbered segment, in the double and the treble of it, he has scored a 'Shanghai' and has automatically won the game.

230 SCRAM

For adults – Any even number – Indoors – Equipment: a darts board and darts.

Each team decides which is the scoring side and which is the 'stopper'. Scorers throw three darts in turn at the board and total their scores. Stoppers throw also, but when they place a dart in any segment, that segment is closed to their opponents. When the stoppers have closed the whole board, the score is totaled and the teams change places.

231 LETTER POSTING

Any age over 6 or 7 – Any number – Indoors – Equipment: several boxes labelled with place names, and for each child pieces of paper bearing all the names.

Before the game starts, hide several boxes around the house with place names written on them. Then give each player several slips of paper with these place names written on them, and tell them to post each 'letter' in the right box. The first player to find all the hidden boxes and post his letters correctly wins the game.

232 PIGGY-BACK TAG

For boys over 7 or 8 – Any number – Outdoors – Equipment: none.

'It' chases all the other players, who are only safe from 'It's' touch if they are riding piggy-back or playing the part of the horse. However, they must dismount and run around on their own when 'It' is nowhere near.

233 SEARCHLIGHTS

Any age over 5 or 6 – Any number – Indoors – Equipment: 2 pencil torches.

The searchlights are held by two players in different corners of a darkened room and are switched on for a count of two only from the searchlight commander. Children creep about in the dark trying to avoid being caught at the tip of a double beam. *Both* beams have to shine on a player's face or head for him to be shot down. All shot-down players go to a neutral corner. If the commander has called for the beams to be put on and a player gets one on him he has to dive fast out of the way before he gets caught by the other one homing in on him. The searchlights can of course get a pattern of aiming together, but this helps the others as well in anticipation.

234 TOWER BRIDGE

Any age over 5 or 6 – Any number – Indoors or outdoors – Equipment: none.

One player stands on his own with his arms outstretched. All other players line up behind him. Odd man out is the bridge, and he lowers his arms from shoulder level down to his sides at any speed he likes. The other players must 'cross the bridge' by passing under his arms without being touched. Anyone touched is out.

235 VOODOO TOUCH

Any age over 5 – Any number – Outdoors – Equipment: none.

'It' is a voodoo witch doctor with the power to paralyse anyone he touches. At his touch, each player freezes and cannot move again until cured by a touch from a free player. This game gets pretty boisterous, but 'It' can win the game by freezing every other player.

236 BUZZ BUZZ

Any age over 5 or 6 – Any number – Indoors or outdoors – Equipment: 2 old hats and 2 blindfolds.

Blindfold two players, give them old hats to wear and stand them at arms' length apart. Neither must move away from this position, but they can duck down at any time. One player says 'Buzz' . . . and the second player must immediately answer with another 'Buzz'. Each player must try to knock the hat off the head of his opponent by a sweeping motion with the flat of his hand. This game is as much fun to watch as to play, but everyone should get a turn. See drawing.

237 UNDER THE TUNNEL RELAY

Any age over 5 or 6 (especially boys) – Any even number – Indoors or outdoors – Equipment: none.

Players form two teams, lined up behind one another. On the starting signal, the first member of each team gets down on his hands and knees and crawls back between the widespread legs of all his team-mates. When he reaches the end he stands up and claps his hand on the shoulder of the next man in the team. That player claps the shoulder of the player in front and so on down the line until the one at the front is tapped. He then crawls down the course – and so on until the whole team has finished. Quickest team wins.

238 CHANGE TAG

Any age over 5 or 6 – Any number – Outdoors – Equipment: none.

Fast and furious, this game is useful for working off excess energy and working up an appetite. Players move around freely while 'It' tries to catch another player. As the players try to avoid him, 'It' can be very crafty and call out the name of another player. This player then becomes 'It's' temporary deputy and can touch other players for him. The confusion just adds to the fun and speeds up the game.

239 ROOSTER FIGHT

Any age over 5 or 6 – Any number in pairs – Outdoors – Equipment: none.

Two opponents take part at a time. Both squat down and hold their ankles. Then, hopping and bumping about, each player tries to make his opponent lose balance or release the grip on his ankles. If he does, he wins the round.

240 JUMP THE STICK RELAY

Any age from 7 or 8 – 2 teams of equal numbers – Outdoors – Equipment: 2 walking sticks or garden canes.

Two teams line up and each leader is given a stick or cane. On the word 'GO' each leader moves down the team, holding the stick out horizontally about a foot above the ground, and each team member jumps over the stick in turn. When the leader reaches the end of the line, the stick is passed back to Number Two in the team, who begins again. The team who finishes first wins. See drawing.

241 BROTHERS

Any age over 4 – Any even number – Indoors – Equipment: a radio or record-player.

Players form two circles with equal numbers in each, one inside the other. Each player chooses a 'brother' in the opposite circle. While a leader plays some music, both circles join hands and skip round in opposite directions. When the music stops, everyone must rush to his 'brother', join hands and sit on the floor. Last pair down are out.

242 CHINESE CHICKEN RACE

Any age over 5 or 6 – Any number – Indoors or outdoors – Equipment: some old books.

This can be played as a team relay or as a fun game for any number of people. Place a line of old books on the floor, about a foot apart. Players squat down with hands crossed on their chest and hop over the books until they reach the end of the line. Then they turn round and hop back. Anyone touching a book or losing his balance is out.

243 COLLECT THE LEAVES

Any age over 7 or 8 – Any even number – Outdoors – Equipment: none, but the game should be played in a garden with trees.

This ideally needs a garden with a varied assortment of trees in it. Each team has a captain who stays at home base ; the rest of the team has to collect, within two minutes and *without talking,* as many different leaves as they can from trees. They must not pick any duplicates – only one oak leaf is allowed, one elm, and so on – as duplicates cancel each other out and do not score. The captain of Team A has to judge Team B and vice versa, so the judging will be tough ! By having a short time limit and absolute silence the risk of duplicates is quite great, since no plan can be worked out – and that rule saves the risk of damage to trees.

244 INDIAN CHIEF

Any age from 5 or 6 – Any number – Indoors – Equipment: none.

Players sit in a circle, facing inwards. One player goes out of the room and an 'Indian Chief' is appointed. He leads the players by performing certain movements, etc. which they must follow. Thus, if he starts humming and clapping his hands together, the rest must do the same. If he suddenly changes this to whistling and stamping feet, the others follow suit.

 The odd man out comes in and walks round behind the seated players. He must try to find out who is the 'Indian Chief'. The other players must keep an eye on their chief so that they can follow when he changes the movements or actions . . . but they must not look at him too obviously or they will give the game away. When Odd Man Out picks out the chief, they change places and start another game.

245 CIRCUS

Any age over 5 or 6 – Any number – Indoors or outdoors – Equipment: record-player or radio, and a ball.

Any number of players form a circle and someone is chosen to be in charge of the music (from a record-player or radio). A ball is passed round the circle from player to player. When the music stops, whoever is holding the ball becomes a circus animal, and must do a little act – with sound effects if possible. Then the music starts again and the game continues until another player is caught with the ball. Each time the music stops, each player must repeat his or her animal trick. When there are ten or so performing seals, trumpeting elephants, roaring lions or chattering monkeys, this game gets pretty noisy . . . but children seem to love it.

246 CIRCLE DODGE

Any age from 5 or 6 – Any number – Outdoors – Equipment: 1 large ball.

Players form two circles, one inside the other. The inside circle joins hands and skips round in a clockwise direction. The circle on the outside have a large ball, and they bowl it along the ground to hit the legs of each player in the inside circle. When a player is hit, he leaves the game. To avoid the ball, they may jump, run or open their legs . . . but they must not break the circle. If this happens, both players who have broken the link are out.

247 SCHOOLTEACHER

Any age over 8 or 9 – Any number – Indoors – Equipment: none.

Players sit in front of the schoolteacher who asks each player in turn such questions as 'Name five towns in France', 'Name five famous composers', 'Five brands of detergent', 'Five capital cities', etc. If a player answers correctly, he moves up one place, if wrong he moves down one place. At the end of the game, whoever is at the top of the class wins.

248 SPELLING BEE

Any age over 7 or 8 – Any number – Indoors – Equipment: a dictionary.

For this you need a person to check the words and a dictionary. Players take turns to spell words. If right, they score a point; if wrong, they lose a point. Start with five points each and vary the words according to the age of the players.

249 ZOO HUNT

Small children – Any even number – Indoors – Equipment: slips of paper bearing animal names.

Write the name of a zoo animal on two slips of paper. The slips are then shuffled up and handed out to players. They must imitate the sound of the animal and join their partner. Noisy, but fun.

250 MUSICAL BUMPS

Small children – Any number – Indoors – Equipment: music.

While music plays, everyone dances around. When it suddenly stops, everyone must quickly sit down on the floor. Last one down is out.

251 BALLOON BANG

Teenagers – Any even number – Indoors or outdoors – Equipment: 2 balloons for each team member, 1 pin for each leader.

Choose two teams and give each player except the team leaders two balloons each. On the starting signal, everyone tries to blow up his balloon as fast as possible. There is one little problem, however; both team leaders are armed with pins and may burst their opponents' balloons. Players with the blown-up balloons must keep running away from the deadly pin. At the end, the team with the most blown-up balloons wins.

252 NUMBER OR YOUR LIFE

Any age over 12 or 13 – Any number – Indoors – Equipment: none.

A leader faces all the other players. He points to any player and calls out a number between one and twelve. The player must immediately shout back a phrase that has a definite association with that number. (An umpire will be useful!) If the player fails, he loses a life and the number is passed on to someone else. Three lives constitute a kill, and the same phrase cannot be used more than once.
　Example
　If the leader called out 'ONE', the player could say: '. . . for the pot', . . . good turn deserves another' or '. . . for all and all for one'.
　For the rest, remember such things as two's company, three's a crowd, four seasons, five-barred gates, seven-league boots, eight arms on an octopus, nine days' wonder, ten commandments, twelve good men and true, etc.

253 CAT AMONG THE PIGEONS

Any age over 4 – Any number – Outdoors – Equipment: none.

Odd man out is the 'cat', and the rest of the players are 'pigeons'. 'Cat' tries to catch 'pigeons' for a feast, but they can fly and he can't. The best that 'cat' can do is to touch a 'pigeon' and clip one of its wings. 'Pigeons' run about flapping their arms until 'cat' touches them. When touched once, 'pigeons' only flap one arm. If touched twice, they stop flapping altogether. Third time touched they are considered as being eaten and are out.

254 BALLOON IN THE BOX

Any age over 6 or 7 – 2 teams of any number – Indoors – Equipment: 2 wastepaper baskets or plastic buckets, balloons, lollipop sticks.

The wastepaper baskets (or buckets) are placed at one end of the room and two teams of competitors line up at the other. Two competitors take part at a time, and are given a balloon and a lollipop stick. On the word 'GO' they must pat the balloon with the stick across the room and get it into the basket. If the balloon touches the floor the competitor is out. The team with the highest score wins.

255 TAKING IN THE WASHING

Any age over 5 or 6 – Any number – Indoors – Equipment: a length of string, about a dozen clothes pins.

Tie each end of the string to a chair back and pin the clothes pins along its length. Each player in turn must collect up as many pins as he can, using one hand only. The player who manages to collect the most without dropping any is the winner.

256 FOX AND GEESE

Any age over 5 or 6 – Any number – Outdoors – Equipment: none.

The 'Geese' move round in file, each one holding the waist of the person in front. Meanwhile an odd man out – the 'Fox' is trying very hard to catch a 'goose'. To do this he must grasp the last 'goose, in the line and count up to five in a loud voice. The leader can drive 'Fox' away before he has finished counting by whipping round to touch him. If the leader isn't quick enough, 'Fox' joins the end of the line and the leader becomes the next 'Fox'.

257 LIONS AND TIGERS

Any age over 5 or 6 – Any number – Indoors – Equipment: none.

The room is divided into two halves and a 'Lion' stands at one end and a 'Tiger' at the other. All other players can move anywhere they like. Both 'Lion' and 'Tiger' try to catch victims, but neither can move into his opponent's half of the room. When either 'animal' catches a victim, they stay in his den. The animal who catches the most players wins.

258 WARS OF THE ROSES

Any age over 7 or 8 – Any number – Indoors – Equipment: collection of assorted small objects.

Divide a room into two halves, and stand a team in each 'territory'. In each 'territory' place a pile of assorted objects, and the two war-

ring sides must sneak into the enemy territory and snatch away the loot. In enemy territory any player can be captured, but if he succeeds in grabbing an object before he is tagged, he may return to his own side. Players need to work together in this game, acting as decoys and luring the enemy across the border line to their doom.

259 BLIND MAN'S HUNT

Teenagers – Any number – Indoors – Equipment: 4 or 5 objects, 2 large paper bags, and 2 blindfolds.

Two volunteers at a time are blindfolded and four or five objects are placed in a line in front of them. They must crawl on hands and knees to the first object, pick it up and return with it to the paper bag at the starting line. They place the object in the bag, turn round and crawl in search of another object. This is fun to watch, as people find it almost impossible to keep any sense of direction when blindfolded. See drawing.

260 CROSSING THE RIVER

Any age over 8 or 9 – Any number – Outdoors – Equipment: a double line of books.

A 'River' is marked out on the lawn with a line of books. It should be about two feet wide at the narrow end, and up to five feet wide at the widest end (according to the age of the children). Players start at the narrow end and do a standing jump over the river and back again. If successful they move further up the river. Anyone who lands in the 'water' drops out, and the last player in wins.

261 OBSTACLES

Any age from 6 or 7 – Any number – Indoors – Equipment: various obstacles.

A volunteer is shown a course marked out with obstacles such as chairs, piles of books, a bowl full of water, etc. He is then blindfolded and told he must walk round the course. As soon as the blindfold is on, the obstacles are quietly removed by the players . . . who then sit back to watch the fun as the blindfolded player steps carefully, trying to avoid non-existent obstacles.

262 BUN BITING

Any age from 5 or 6 – Small numbers at a time – Indoors – Equipment: a bun on a string for each competitor.

Suspend some buns on pieces of string from the top of a door. Competitors then race to be the first to eat a bun, without touching it with their hands.

263 PENNY IN THE SQUARE

Any age over 6 or 7 — Any even number — Indoors — Equipment: adhesive tape, a soft ball and a penny.

This is a game played on an elimination basis. Mark out a ten-inch square on the floor with adhesive tape and place a penny in the centre. Stand the first two competitors opposite each other three feet away from the square. Give them a soft ball, and tell them to knock the penny out of the circle by bouncing the ball to each other and hitting the penny in the square on the bounce. When the first penny has been knocked out of the square, the successful 'ball bouncer' takes on the next challenger.

264 BOOT BAGATELLE

Any age over 6 or 7 — Any number, in groups — Indoors — Equipment: 3 pairs of shoes, and 3 table tennis balls for each contestant.

Place three pairs of shoes in a line on the floor with the toes of the shoes pointing away from the players. Stand the contestants several feet away armed with three table tennis balls. The contestants must try to throw the ball into a shoe. The player throwing the most in is the winner. If more than one person scores the same, move the shoes further away.

265 DUMB CRAMBO

Any age over 6 or 7 — Any even number — Indoors — Equipment: none.

Players form two teams. One team goes out while the other decides upon a word. When the outside team comes back, they are told a word that rhymes with the actual one chosen. Then they are given a little mime to illustrate the chosen word and are allowed three guesses. Only members of the guessing team are allowed to speak.

266 FEATHER RELAY RACE

Any age over 7 or 8 — Teams of 4 — Indoors — Equipment: 1 feather.

Select teams of four and give each team a feather. Each team leader starts from one wall of the room and blows the feather as far as he can with one puff. The second player blows the feather on again. Both teams are aiming for the opposite wall, but as feathers tend to blow this way and that, this is not as easy as it sounds. When all four team members have had a blow, the team nearest the finishing wall wins.

267 FINGER SPOOF

Any age over 7 or 8 — Any number, in pairs — Indoors — Equipment: none.

Two contestants face each other across a table. Both have their right hands clenched and held in the air. On the word 'GO' from the referee both players throw their hands down on the table, extending any number of fingers as they do so, and each player shouts a guess as to how many fingers will be shown. The first correct guess wins . . . or if playing in teams, scores one point for that team.

268 TARGET BOUNCE

Any age from 6 or 7 – Any number in groups – Indoors – Equipment: egg carton or cartons, ping pong balls.

Place an egg carton on the floor, stand the players about six feet away, and give them ping pong balls to bounce off the floor and into one of the egg compartments. See drawing.

269 HANDCLAP

Any age over 5 or 6 – Any number, in pairs – Indoors – Equipment: none.

Two contestants stand facing each other, and at the same time, start the following little ritual :
 Slap right hand against opponent's right palm; slap own palms together; slap left palm against opponent's left palm; slap own palms together; slap both palms against opponent's; slap own hands against thighs.
 The first contestant to slap own thighs wins the round. A sharp-eyed judge will be needed for this one.

270 LITTLE CLOWN

Small children – Any number – Indoors – Equipment: none.

All players join hands, except for one child who is 'The Little Clown'. While the children join hands and dance round the clown, they sing this song to the tune of 'Here we go round the Mulberry Bush' :

Oh, here comes the Little Clown,
The Little Clown, the Little Clown,
Oh, here comes the Little Clown
Let's copy what he's doing.

 When the song is finished, the players clap loudly and wait for The Little Clown to do something. Whatever the clown does, the children imitate. Each child should get a turn in the centre as the clown.

94

271 BUSY BEE

Small children — Any number — Indoors or outdoors — Equipment: none.

Pair the children off, and choose a leader to call out different commands, such as: 'Stand back to back', or: 'Stand side by side'. However, when the leader calls out: 'Busy Bees', the children buzz round the room and seek a different partner. The leader also tries to take one of the partners by touching him and the odd man out gives the next set of commands.

272 COBBLER, COBBLER

Any age over 4 — Any number — Indoors — Equipment: 1 slipper.

Players sit on the floor in a tight circle with 'It' in the middle. A soft slipper is passed round the circle, behind the backs of the players. The children chant the following little rhyme.

      Cobbler, cobbler, mend my shoe,
      Have it done by half past two.
'It' then puts his hands over his eyes and says:
      Cobbler, cobbler, tell me true,
      Which of you has got my shoe?
When he reaches the word 'shoe', the person holding the slipper keeps it behind his back. 'It' looks at all the faces and tries to guess who has the slipper. He has two guesses and if he finds the right one, the player takes 'Its' place in the centre.

273 WOBBLING BUNNIES

Any age over 4 – Any number – Indoors or outdoors – Equipment: none.

All the children crouch down and pretend to be rabbits. They hop and jump all over the room, or lawn, holding their hands up by the side of their faces like a rabbit's ears. When the leader calls out 'HUNTER' all the rabbits must freeze exactly where they are while the leader counts slowly up to five. Any 'bunny' who wobbles or loses balance while the leader is counting goes out.

274 JOHNNIE'S LOST HIS TROUSERS

Any age over 4 – Any number – Indoors – Equipment: none.

Children sit in a circle with the leader in the middle. The leader chants the following:

> Johnnie's lost his trousers,
> Johnnie's lost his trousers,
> I think I know who's taken them,
> It's YOU.

With that, the leader points accusingly to one of the players, who must not speak, nor smile. That player must deny the accusation by vigorously shaking his head and quickly pointing to another player. Each player denies the charge and points out someone else. Any child who smiles, speaks or does not deny the accusation quickly is out.

275 MUSCLES

Any age over 8 or 9 – Any even number – Outdoors – Equipment: a piece of wood, nails and 2 hammers.

Take a thick old plank of wood and tap a 5-inch nail lightly into it at each end. Each team is given one hammer and each player is allowed one tap at a time. The first to get the nail completely in is the winner. The judge must insist on only one tap per person at least until it is his turn again – for just one tap. Nail lengths and wood thicknesses can of course be varied according to the ages of the players. If the nail flattens over a new one has to be started – this rule helps give the less muscular a chance!

276 PACK SHUFFLE

Icebreaker – Any age over 5 or 6 – 4 equal teams – Indoors – Equipment: a pack of cards.

Place a pack of playing cards face down on the floor, and place four chairs in a row about ten feet away. Then sort the players into four equal teams. Each player in turn walks up to the pack of cards and picks up a card. The first player to pick up a King shouts out whatever it is – say, 'King of Spades' – and sits down on one of the chairs. The Queen of Spades must sit on his lap, the Jack sits on the Queen's lap . . . and so on. All players must follow only in the correct suit and form new teams. The first complete suit brings the game to an end.

If you wish, sort out the cards first so that only the King, Queen, Jack and Ten are on the floor. Then you will only have finished teams of four.

277 MAKE A RHYME

Any age over 8 or 9 – Any number – Indoors – Equipment: none.

Players sit around in a circle, with a leader in the centre. The leader says:

> I want a rhyme in jolly quick time,
> And the word I choose is . . .

Whatever word the leader chooses, each player in turn must give a rhyming word for it. The first person to fault drops out. The leader can always be challenged himself by any player, so he can't use difficult words that he might not be able to rhyme himself.

278 BLIND MAN'S BATTLE

Any age over 6 or 7 – Any number, in pairs – Indoors or outdoors – Equipment: 2 rolled up newspapers 2 blindfolds.

This is a game for two blindfolded players at a time, each armed with a rolled-up newspaper. The two contestants lie down on the floor on their stomachs, facing each other. Each player says in turn: 'Where are you ?' His opponent says: 'Here I am' — and immediately rolls to a different position. The first player lets fly with his roll of newspaper, attempting to land a blow on his opponent's left shoe. The first player to land a clean tap on his partner's left shoe is the winner.

279 BIGAMY

Teenagers or adults — Ideally, more girls than boys (see below) — Indoors — Equipment: radio or record-player.

Arrange chairs in sets of three. On each set a boy sits between two girls, except for one set, upon which sits a boy with only one 'wife'. His other chair is empty. While music plays, the boy with only one 'wife' grabs her by the hand and runs to collect another. The boy who has just been robbed of one of his wives does likewise . . . and so on. When the music suddenly stops, the boy with only one wife retires from the game, taking his wife and three chairs with him.

280 SHOOT THE DICE·

Any age over 6 or 7 — Any number — Indoors — Equipment: 1 die, 1 tennis ball.

Players form a large circle, in the centre of which is a die. Using a tennis ball, each player in turn bowls at the die. If he hits it, he scores the number of points shown when it comes to rest. If he misses, he subtracts from his score the number already showing on the die. Highest score out of three turns wins.

281 JUNIOR PAUL JONES

Icebreaker — Any age over 10 or 11 — Equal numbers of girls and boys — Indoors — Equipment: a radio or record-player.

This is a useful game to play if the guests do not know each other very well. Two circles are formed, one inside the other. Girls are in one circle, boys in another. Both circles dance round in opposite directions while music is playing. When the music stops, the boy must turn to his opposite number and ask her name, her likes and dislikes, etc. Continue the game until everyone has spoken to at least half a dozen others.

282 MUSICAL CROCODILE

Icebreaker — Any age over 8 or 9 — Any number — Indoors — Equipment: none.

Everyone sits down except the leader, who marches round the room singing 'John Brown's Body'. When he's finished the verse, he picks out one of the seated players, who grasps him round the waist and walks round with him while they both sing again. After every verse and chorus, another player joins on until everyone is walking round in a 'crocodile' and singing together.

283 MUSICAL FLASHLIGHT

Any age over 9 or 10 — Any number — Indoors — Equipment: one flashlight.

As this game is played with the lights out, it is ideal for Hallow'een parties. A leader takes charge of the music (with a radio or record player) and the rest of the players stand in a circle. A flashlight is handed round from player to player, each person holding it just under his chin for a moment to light up his face in a rather eerie manner. Whoever is holding the flashlight when the music stops is out.

284 CHOPSTICKS RELAY

Any age over 8 or 9 — Teams of equal numbers — Indoors — Equipment: 2 cocktail sticks, 2 egg cups and 5 dried peas per team.

Each team is given two cocktail sticks and two egg cups. In one egg cup are five dried peas. Using only the cocktail sticks as chopsticks, the first player of each team transfers all the dried peas to the second egg cup, then the next player moves them back. First team to finish wins. The game can also be played with unsharpened pencils instead of cocktail sticks.

285 MIXED OBJECT RELAY

Any age over 8 or 9. — Teams of equal numbers — Indoors — Equipment: 2 identical collections of assorted objects.

Two identical piles of assorted objects are placed on the floor in front of the teams. These objects should be awkward and dissimilar in shape and the total pile should be difficult to pick up and carry in two hands. Some suggestions: empty cigarette packets, two ping pong balls, pencils, clothes pins, etc. The teams play a relay race in which each player scoops up all the objects, runs round the room and then drops all the objects on the floor in front of the next player. If a player drops a single object he must stop to pick it up.

286 POTATO PUPPETS

Any age from 5 or 6 — Any number — Indoors — Equipment: 1 large potato, some matches, a pencil and strands of wool for each player.

Competitors are given one large potato, a few matches, a pencil, and some strands of wool. In two minutes, they must make a potato puppet head. The best or funniest puppet wins the prize.

287 MYSTERY WHISTLE

Any age over 7 or 8 – Any number – Indoors – Equipment: a blindfold, a whistle tied to a length of string, a safety pin.

Halfway between a trick and a game, Mystery Whistle only works once, but you can spin it out by choosing three or four victims who are sent out of the room. One victim comes in at a time and is blindfolded. While the blindfold is being placed on the victim, something else is going on behind his back. An ordinary whistle, tied to a long piece of string, is being pinned to his back.

The victim is now told that he has to find the person with the whistle. The blindfold is removed, and players gather round the victim in a circle. One of the players reaches forward gently and lifts the whistle tied to the victim's back. He blows it and then quickly but gently lets it dangle back. The victim whirls round to confront the whistle-blower. Now the player who is nearest to the whistle repeats the performance – and the victim hears the whistle blow on the other side of the circle.

It can be quite a long time before the luckless victim realises that the whistle is on his own back.

288 WILDEST DREAM

Adults – Any number – Indoors – Equipment: none.

Each player in turn thinks about his 'wildest dream' (such as winning a fortune on the football pools, flying a jumbo jet plane, etc.).

Other players have to guess what that dream is by asking only twenty questions. An enlightening game sometimes, revealing many secrets about your guests.

289 PENCIL TWIST RELAY

Any age over 6 or 7 – Teams of equal numbers – Indoors – Equipment: 4 pencils and 2 pieces of string per team.

Four pencils and two pieces of string exactly the same length are needed. A pencil is tied to each end of the two pieces of string. Two teams are formed and the first player of each picks up a pencil and winds up the string by twisting it round and round. When the two pencils touch, he unwinds the string again and passes it to the second player in his team. The first team to wind and unwind the string wins the race.

290 STEPPING STONE RACE

Any age over 6 or 7 – Teams of 2 to 6 players – Indoors – Equipment: 2 books per team.

This can be played as a team relay or as a race for two to six players at a time. Each player (or each team) is given two old books. At the word 'GO' they must place one book on the ground, step on to it, move their second book forward, step on to that, then turn round to retrieve the first book. The course must be completed stepping only on the books. If a player's foot touches the floor, he goes back to the start.

291 BOTTLE BALANCE RELAY

Any age over 6 or 7 – Teams of equal numbers – Indoors – Equipment: 2 empty milk bottles.

Stand two milk bottles at one end of the course, right way up. The first team members run to the bottle, and balance it upside down (on its neck). Then they rush back and the second member runs up, stands the bottle right way up . . . and so on. If a bottle fails to balance as a player is racing back to his team he must go back and stand it up properly.

292 OVER THE LINE RELAY

Any age over 8 or 9 – Any even number – Outdoors – Equipment: tape to mark the finishing line.

Line up two teams of players, with the tallest in the front and the smallest at the back. On the word 'GO' the second person in each line vaults the first and is carried piggy back over a line so many yards away. Then Number Four in the line vaults on to the back of Number Three, and is taken piggy back style over the line. The same method is continued until the first team to have carried all their players over the line become the winners.

293 MUSICAL GROUPS

Any age over 5 or 6 – Any number – Indoors – Equipment: a radio or record-player.

A leader plays music while all the players move around the room. When the music stops, the leader calls out a number and the players must quickly form themselves into groups of that exact number. So if the leader calls out: 'Five', all the players must form groups of five. The leader makes it more fun by calling numbers that are bound to leave a few players unable to form a complete group. These unlucky ones go out of the game.

294 BALLOON HANDICAP

Any age over 6 or 7 – Teams of equal numbers – Indoors – Equipment: an unsharpened pencil for each player, balloons.

Form the players into two teams and give each person an un- sharpened pencil. Indicate a goal area at each end of the room. By tapping a balloon with their pencils only, each team must try to score in its opponent's goal. Players must not touch the balloon with their hands or allow it to drop to the floor – if they do, a penalty 'tap' is awarded to the opposing team. First team to score 3 goals wins the match.

295 ORCHESTRAS

Icebreaker – Any age over 5 or 6 – Any even number – Indoors – Equipment: as listed or as available.

Each team is given a comb, one piece of tissue paper, beans, empty canisters, elastic bands, hairpins, pencils and string and has to make music with them. The orchestra has to be ready to start within two minutes from the word 'GO'. A classical tune such as 'Yankee Doodle' or similar has to be played as the set piece. Best performance (no rehearsals allowed) wins. But even if nobody wins, everybody has fun.

296 THE WORLD'S WORST JOKE

Adults – Any number – Indoors – Equipment: none.

A simple one, this, but a good quickie. Each person tells a joke, and the one greeted by the loudest groans wins the contest.

297 CAT ON THE MAT

Any age from 5 or 6 – Any number – Indoors – Equipment: several paper 'mats' and music.

Several sheets of paper (signifying 'mats') are placed around the floor in a rough circle. The players dance round and must step on every mat whenever they are near one. A leader plays music and stops it at any time. When the music stops, everyone freezes where they are. Any 'cat' who is caught out standing on a 'mat' is out of the game.

298 LIFEBOATS

Any age from 5 or 6 – Any number – Indoors – Equipment: several sheets of paper, and music.

When you have played Cat on the Mat, try this game as a variation. While music is playing, the children move round, preferably some distance away from 'lifeboats' (the sheets of paper). When the music stops, players must try to stand on one of the papers . . . but no more than two players may use any one lifeboat. If they do, it 'sinks', and the players are sent off. Anyone who fails to find a lifeboat is 'out' and one of the lifeboats is removed.

299 ANAGRAMS

Any age over 10 or 11 – Any number – Indoors – Equipment: a list of identical jumbled words and a pencil for each player.

Players are given identical lists of words which have their letters all jumbled up. The first to rearrange all the words in their proper form wins.

300 ODD MAN OUT

Any age over 10 or 11 — Any number — Indoors — Equipment: identical list of objects and pencil for each player.

Each player is given a list of objects or names, in which one is the 'odd man out'. The player who discovers most in a set time wins.

Examples: Apple, Orange, Plum, Potato, Pear, Pineapple. (POTATO is odd — a vegetable and all the others are fruits.)

Red, Green, Blue, Yellow. (GREEN is odd — because it is not a primary colour.)

301 KNEE BOXING

Any age over 5 or 6 — Any number of pairs — Indoors or outdoors — Equipment: none.

Partners face each other, crouching slightly. Either may move or jump out of the way, but the trick is to slap the opponent's knees with the flat of the hands. Not as easy as it sounds when each player is trying to do the very same thing. Three hits constitute a win.

302 PEEL PORTRAITS

Any age over 7 or 8 — Any number — Indoors — Equipment: pieces of peel, a large salad bowl and a sheet of paper for each player.

Pieces of peel left from a salad are put into a bowl. Each player is then given a sheet of paper and asked to make a face using only peel. The peel can be bent or broken as the artist wishes, and the funniest face wins.

303 HOPPING FIGHT

Any age over 5 or 6 — Any number of pairs — Indoors or outdoors — Equipment: none.

Partners stand on one foot within touching distance of one another and then each must try to force his opponent to place both feet on the ground, but only pushes with the flat of the hand are allowed.

304 HOP AND PULL

Any age over 5 or 6 — Any number of pairs — Indoors or outdoors — Equipment: none.

A variation of Hopping Fight. Partners clasp hands and try to make each other lift one foot off the ground just by pulling. See drawing.

305 FOOT TRAP

Any age over 6 or 7 – Any number of pairs – Indoors or outdoors –
Equipment: none.

Everyone's shoes should be taken off for this game. Partners face one another at arm's length, and then each player tries to place both feet over those of his opponent. When one player is successful in placing his foot over one of his opponent's, the two feet touching are out of play and cannot be moved. The second half of the game is far more difficult and great fun to watch. If the game is a draw, it is replayed until one player wins with both feet.

306 THE SPONGE RACE

Any age over 6 or 7 – About 6 players – Indoors – Equipment: plastic
tablecloth or a few sheets of newspaper, a bowl of water, and a paper
cup and a small piece of sponge for each player.

Cover a table with the plastic cloth or newspaper and stand on it a bowl of water and a paper cup for each player. Each competitor is given a piece of sponge and has to fill his cup with water by dipping his sponge in the bowl and squeezing it out over his cup. First one to fill his cup is the winner.

307 ROUNDABOUT TOUCH

Any age over 5 or 6 – Any number – Outdoors – Equipment: none.

Players form a circle and hold hands, and one person who is 'It' stands outside the circle.

'It' calls the name of any player and tries to touch him on the shoulder. The named player pulls everyone round with him trying to avoid 'It's' touch and changes direction from clockwise to anticlockwise as he likes. All players in the circle help to defeat 'It'. If 'It' touches the wrong person twice, another player takes his place.

308 SWAMP

Any age over 5 or 6 – Any number – Indoors or outdoors – Equipment: a newspaper.

Players form a circle, holding hands. In the centre is a spread out newspaper. This is the deadly swamp, and any player touching it is doomed to be sent out of the game. It's a case of everyone against everyone as each player pulls and twists in an effort to make someone else tread on the swamp.

309 ROAR, LION, ROAR

Any age over 4 – Any number – Indoors or outdoors – Equipment: 1 blindfold.

This is a variation on the popular game called Squeak, Piggy, Squeak. While the other players form a circle round him, 'It' is blindfolded and turned round three times. When 'It' stops, he points at a player and says: 'Roar, Lion, Roar'. The player pointed at has to imitate a lion's roar and 'It' has to identify him. If successful, he changes places with the 'lion'.

310 PAT-A-CAKE

Small children – Any number – Indoors – Equipment: none, but someone must lead the singing.

Pat-a-cake, pat-a-cake, baker's man
            (*Children clap hands*).
Bake me a cake as fast as you can
            (*They wave their hands quickly in the air*).
Pat it and prick it, and mark it with 'B'
            (*The children mime these actions and outline
            the letter 'B' in the air*).
And bake in the oven for baby and me.
            (*They pretend to place the cake in an oven and
            close the door*).

311 SING A SONG OF SIXPENCE

Small children — Any number — Indoors — Equipment: none, but someone must lead the singing.

Sing a song of sixpence,
> (*Children describe a figure 6 in the air*)

A pocket full of rye
> (*They empty out pockets*)

Four-and-twenty blackbirds
> (*Flapping arms, and general bird imitations*)

Baked in a pie.
> (*Mime of pie being made*)

When the pie was opened
> (*They pretend to cut pie*)

The birds began to sing
> (*Cue for children to go mad with bird imitations*)

Wasn't that a dainty dish
To set before a king ?
> (*Mime of placing pie on table*)

The King was in his counting house
Counting out his money ;
> (*Children mime counting of a pile of coins*).

The Queen was in the parlour
Eating bread and honey ;
> (*Mime of eating*).

The maid was in the garden
Hanging out the clothes
> (*Mime of someone hanging washing on a line*).

When down came a blackbird
And pecked off her nose.
> (*Mime of swooping bird, then children hold their noses with expression of pain*).

312 LITTLE MISS MUFFET

Small children — Any number — Indoors — Equipment: none, but someone must lead the singing.

Little Miss Muffet
Sat on a Tuffet
> (*Children sit down*).

Eating her curds and whey,
> (*Pretend to eat with a spoon from a bowl*).

Along came a spider
> (*Children do spider imitations*).

Who sat down beside her
  (*Mime of spider frightening Miss Muffet*).
And frightened Miss Muffet away.
  (*Children look scared and pretend to run away*).

313 MULBERRY BUSH

Small children – Any number – Indoors – Equipment: none.

The children join hands and run round in a circle while singing the words of this old favourite. They mime the actions of the song in each verse, then join hands and run round again for the chorus.

Here we go round the mulberry bush,
The mulberry bush, the mulberry bush,
Here we go round the mulberry bush,
On a cold and frosty morning.
This is the way we wash our clothes,
Wash our clothes, wash our clothes,
This is the way we wash our clothes,
On a cold a frosty morning.
Here we go round the mulberry bush ...

Other Verses

This is the way we iron our clothes ..

This is the way we darn our socks...
This is the way we brush our teeth...
This is the way we walk to school...
This is the way we comb our hair...
This is the way we scrub the floor...
This is the way we dance and sing...

314 THREE BLIND MICE

Small children – Any number – Indoors – Equipment: none.

The children hold hands and form a circle, with one child in the middle playing 'The Farmer's Wife'.
   They dance round, singing the song:
   Three blind mice,
   Three blind mice.
   See how they run,
   See how they run.
   They all ran after the farmer's wife
   Who cut off their tails with a carving knife.
   Did you ever see such a thing in your life
   As three blind mice?
   On the last word, 'mice', the children break hands and rush for the nearest wall. 'The Farmer's Wife' must try to catch the players before they touch the wall. The first one caught becomes the next 'Farmer's Wife'.

315 SQUIRRELS

Any age over 4 – Any odd number – Indoors or outdoors – Equipment: none.

The children, in pairs, face each other with their hands clasped above their heads. They are hollow trees, and each tree is a home for a child playing a squirrel. He crouches behind his own tree. One extra player is a squirrel without a tree.
   This player shouts: 'Hunt for nuts', and all the squirrels must come out of their trees and change homes. The odd squirrel takes this chance to sneak behind one of the trees. The next homeless squirrel continues the game. The squirrels change places with the trees at least once during the game.

316 POOR PUSSY

Any age over 4 – Any number – Indoors or outdoors – Equipment: none.

Children gather in a circle and surround the 'pussy' who sits down. Each child pats the 'pussy' on the head, or strokes it, while murmuring 'poor pussy, poor pussy'.

'Pussy' makes mewing and purring noises, and makes faces at all the players. The first player to smile or laugh takes 'pussy's' place in the middle.

317 MAGICIAN

Any age over 4 — Any number — Indoors or outdoors — Equipment: a ruler or short cane to be used as a wand.

A simple game this. The only equipment you really need is a set of ear-plugs for every adult within two miles. One child is appointed as the Magician, given a magic wand and set loose among all the other players. He turns them into cars, trains, planes, goats, frogs, rabbits . . in fact anything, by pointing at each in turn with his wand, and watches as they make noises and actions appropriate to their roles. The best performance wins the wand for the next game.

318 THE WITCH'S CAT

Any age over 7 or 8 — Any number— Indoors — Equipment: none.

Children take turns to give an adjective and a name to the Witch's cat . . . but both must begin with the same letter of the alphabet.
    For instance, the first player might say: 'The witch's cat is an ANGRY cat and her name is ANGELA.' The second player says : 'The witch's cat is a BEAUTIFUL cat and her name is BETTY'. The third player takes the letter 'C' and could say : 'The witch's cat is a CHEER-FUL cat and his name is CHARLIE'. And so on. Anyone who hesitates or gives a word beginning with the wrong letter is out. You can make the game more difficult by stating that no names or adjectives may be used twice. Best played very fast.

319 CROSSWORD PUZZLE

Any age over 10 or 11 — Up to 6 players — Indoors — Equipment: pencil and paper for each player.

All players take a pencil and paper and mark out a blank crossword pattern, five squares by five. Then in order, each player calls out a letter, which everyone must place somewhere in his squares. The object of the game is to make as many five letter words — up, down or across as possible — so every player makes sure to call out a letter he has a use for. No cheating on this . . . everyone MUST use all the letters that are called out.

320 CARD FLICKING

Any age over 7 or 8 — Any number — Indoors — Equipment: packs of old playing cards.

Deal playing cards out equally between all players. They stand on a line about ten feet from a wall and flick one card at a time towards the wall. If one player's card lands on any part of another, he wins all the cards on the floor at that time. The eventual winner is the player who ends up with the most cards.

321 CLOTHES PIN TARGET

Any age over 8 or 9 — Any number — Indoors — Equipment: a milk bottle and 6 clothes pins.

The idea is that each player takes it in turn to drop the clothes pins, one by one, into the milk bottle, and the player with the highest score wins. Each player stands with both feet together, and the bottle is placed about three inches in front of his toes. He must bring the pins up level with his chin, and drop them from that height, keeping his body erect and bending his head only.

322 BETWEEN THE SHOALS

Any age over 6 or 7 — Any number of pairs — Indoors — Equipment: 2 pencils and 1 piece of paper for each pair.

Divide a sheet of paper into three equal sections. The central zone is neutral ground.

Taking pencils, each player marks an 'X' (which represents his base) and ten small circles (which are defences). Each player takes a turn, starting from his own 'X', to draw a single, quick slashing straight line towards the 'X' of his opponent. Every defensive circle he crosses counts as a point against him, but he scores five points if he hits his opponent's 'X'. See drawing.

323 CARDS IN THE BUCKET

Any age over 7 or 8 – Any even number – Indoors or outdoors – Equipment: a bucket and an old pack of cards.

Take a plastic bucket and a pack of old playing cards. Choose two teams and give the pack of fifty-two cards to one. Deal the cards out equally, stand the teams about six feet away from the bucket and let one team try to throw their cards into the bucket. The 'hits' are counted and then the second team has a go. The team with most cards in the bucket wins.

324 WORD SPLITTING

Any age over 9 or 10 – Any number – Indoors – Equipment: pencils and paper for each player.

All competitors are given paper and pencils and one fairly long word. In five minutes, they must make as many words as they can from the given word. The person with the most proper and correctly spelled words wins.

325 CONSEQUENCES

Any age over 9 or 10 – Any number – Indoors – Equipment: paper and pencils.

The leader passes a sheet of paper to the first player and says: 'Write down a boy's name'. When he's done that, the paper is folded so that the next player cannot see what has been written, and is passed on to the next. To that player, the leader says: 'This boy met a girl . . . write down her name'. The paper is then folded again and passed on to a third player.

The leader says: 'Write down where they met'. To the next, the leader says: 'What was the boy wearing?' . . . then: 'What was the girl wearing?' . . . and so on until all players have had a part in making up a complete story. Then the slip of paper is unfolded and the results are read out, the reader filling in connecting words as necessary.

A typical story could run something like this:

Johnny Bragg met Deirdre Smith in the desert. Johnny was wearing a raincoat and Deirdre Smith was wearing a bikini and football boots. She said: 'I'd like to go dancing'. He said: 'I'll take you to the zoo'. So they went to the aquarium and had several drinks.

326 GUESS THE PLACE

Icebreaker – Adults – Any number – Indoors – Equipment: pictures of castles, etc., plus pencils and paper.

From picture-postcards, old magazines, travel brochures etc., cut out pictures of well-known landmarks, such as castles and bridges. Players have a pencil and paper and try to list as many of the places as they can. The player with the most correct wins.

327 MATCHING PAIRS

Icebreaker – Any age over 8 or 9 – Any even number – Indoors – Equipment: 1 card cut in 2 for each pair.

A useful game for helping to introduce party guests to each other.

For each two guests, take a postcard or a square of stiff paper and cut in two, with a different pattern for each one. Each half is placed in an envelope and one half given to each guest. They have to find who has the matching piece of their pattern. Where necessary, keep one half for boys and the other for girls – a good way to mix the sexes.

328 SOUL MATES

Icebreaker – Any age over 8 or 9 – Any even number of boys and girls – Indoors – Equipment: 1 slip of paper for each, bearing male and female names.

Another 'matching' game for pairing off party guests. Take slips of paper and on each write half of a famous pair. For instance, Antony and Cleopatra, Darby and Joan, Romeo and Juliet, Samson and Delilah, Hiawatha and Minehaha, Adam and Eve. One male name is given to each boy and a female name to each girl. They must then find their partners.

329 ONE-MINUTE WORD QUIZ

Any age over 11 or 12 — Any number — Indoors — Equipment: a pencil and paper for each player.

Players are given a minute to write down as many words as they can beginning and ending with the same letter. The longest list wins.
  Examples: Tent, Test, Libel, Rubber, Cynic.

330 HANGMAN

Any age over 7 or 8 — 2 teams of even numbers — Indoors — Equipment: blackboard and chalk, or large sheet of paper and a pencil.

A blackboard, or large sheet of paper, is required for this game. Choose two teams and one team selects a certain word — preferably with six letters or more.
  The leader of the first team then draws the appropriate number of dashes on the blackboard. Members of the opposing team now have to fill in the letters of the mystery word. If they suggest a correct letter, then the team leader must fill it in. If, however, they mention a letter which does not appear in the mystery word, the team leader draws the first part of the hanging man, and writes the incorrect letter at the foot of the board.
  All through the game, the first team add a new part to the hanging man each time the opposing team say a wrong letter. If the hanging man is completed, the opposing team have lost the game. If they guess the word before the drawing is finished, they win the game.
  The correct moves (in order) for the hanging man are as follows: (1) The gallows and rope, (2) The head, (3) The body, (4) The face, (5) One arm, (6) Second arm, (7) One leg, (8) Second leg, (9) One foot, (10) Second foot. See drawing.

331 HARD SENTENCE

Any age over 11 or 12 — Any number — Indoors — Equipment: a pencil and a list of words for each player.

Players are given a list of six unlikely words, chosen at random. The first to write down a readable sentence using all of them wins the game.

332 THE STORY-SPINNING GAME

Any age over 11 or 12 — Any number — Indoors — Equipment: a ball of string.

This is fun to play, but needs a little advance preparation. Take a ball of string, and cut a length of about four feet for each player. Knot the lengths together and rewind them into a ball. Seat the players in a circle, and hand the ball to one of them. He must begin a story and, unwinding the ball as he goes, continue it until he reaches the first knot. He then passes the ball to the next player, who must keep the story going until he reaches the second knot. He hands on to the next player, and so on. The more weird or outrageous the story becomes, the better !

333 SENTENCES

Any age over 11 or 12 — Any number — Indoors — Equipment: pencil and paper for each player.

Contestants write the longest sentences they can using only words containing a certain number of letters — say three, four or five. Or, they can write a long sentence using no word of more than four letters.

334 JUMBLED TOWNS

Any age over 10 or 11 — Any number — Indoors — Equipment: lists of jumbled town names and pencils.

Players are given sheets of paper and pencils and lists of jumbled names of towns. After two minutes, the player with the most right wins.
  Some examples: YOWNERK/NEW YORK; MINBMAHRIG/BIRMINGHAM; ERMO/ROME; STOBNO/BOSTON; STOUHON/HOUSTON; LENON SEWAR/NEW ORLEANS.

335 FIRST NAMES

Any age over 9 or 10 – Any number – Indoors – Equipment: lists of famous last names and pencils for each child.

Players are given a list of famous last names, of people living or dead. In two minutes, each player must supply as many of the first names as possible.

336 BALLOON BURST

Any age over 8 or 9 – Any number – Outdoors – Equipment: plenty of balloons.

Either played as a straightforward race or as a team game, this game consists merely of blowing a balloon up until it bursts. Not for the faint-hearted.

337 BUNNY-HOP TAG

Any age over 4 – Any number – Outdoors – Equipment: none.

The old tag game, in which 'It' tries to catch all the others, with the added difficulty of everyone being allowed to move only with rabbit-like hops.

338 LOOT

Any age over 9 or 10 – Any number – Outdoors – Equipment: 1 large ball.

'It' tries to catch the robber who is carrying away his loot . . . in the form of a large ball which players throw from one to another. 'It' has to catch the person actually holding the ball, and if successful, changes places with him.

339 PING PONG PITCH

Any age over 7 or 8 – Any number – Outdoors – Equipment: a bucket, and 4 ping pong balls.

Put a bucket on its side and give each competitor in turn four ping pong balls. From a distance of six to eight feet, they must try to get the ping pong balls in the bucket. If they throw too hard, the ball will bounce out and if they don't throw hard enough the ball won't even get there. The person with the highest score wins.

340 KNEE-BALL RELAY

Any age over 8 or 9 – Any number – Outdoors – Equipment: 2 beach balls, 2 books.

A relay race for two teams, in which they race across the room carrying a beach ball between their knees and a book on their head, neither of which may be dropped without starting again.

341 DUETS

Any age over 6 or 7 – Any even number – Indoors – Equipment: a song book or a list of song lyrics.

Two teams pair off in opposition. Each pair has to sing a different song at the same time – for example, one may have to sing 'John Brown's Body' while the other sings 'Oh! Susanna'. Neither is allowed to laugh or smile during the performance and the person who gets through best without a smile wins the round. The others meanwhile judge, with the host having a casting vote. Winners of the round go on to a grand final with the opposition pulling faces to make them laugh. Words typed in advance can get this going smoothly.

342 BIG HEAD, BIG FEET

Adults – Any number – Indoors – Equipment: paper and a pencil.

Each man writes his hat and shoe size on a slip of paper and hands it to his host. A complete list is then drawn up by the host, and everyone has to guess which sizes belong to which man. The first person to guess accurately the hat and shoe size of a fellow-guest is the winner.

343 ROCKET RACE

Any age over 8 or 9 – Any number – Indoors – Equipment: a fancy shaped balloon for each player.

Competitors are given a balloon each . . . preferably a spiral or fancy type. They stand at one end of the room, blow up their balloons, point them towards the other wall and let fly. The player whose balloon travels furthest wins. A burst balloon knocks the competitor out of the game.

344 MATCHING WORDS

Any age from 8 or 9 – Any number – Indoors – Equipment: pencil and paper for each player.

Players sit down with a pencil and paper and the leader reels off a list of words that have a well-known matching word. The player who writes down the most matching words wins.

Some examples of matching words: Black – and White; Odd – and Even; Jack – and Jill; Adam – and Eve; Hide – and Seek; Soap – and Water; Cats – and Dogs; Bacon – and Eggs.

345 THIS IS MY NOSE

Any age from 6 or 7 – Any number – Indoors – Equipment: none.

Everyone lines up facing the leader, who points to her left ear and says 'This is my nose'. The players must quickly reverse this mix up, point to their noses and shout. 'This is my left ear'. Anyone who gets it wrong is sent off. Then the leader points to her foot and says: 'This is my chin' . . . whereupon other players would point to their chins and say: 'This is my foot', etc.

346 MISSING PERSONS

Any age from 9 or 10 – Any number – Indoors – Equipment: none.

All the players sit on the floor in a circle and 'It' is sent out of the room. While 'It' is outside, one of the seated players disappears either by hiding or by going out of a different door. When 'It' comes in, he has twenty seconds to name the missing person. (This is not easy when twenty or so people are taking part.)

347 INDOOR BALLOON BALL

Any age over 6 or 7 — Any even number — Indoors — Equipment: a balloon (but keep some extras).

Two teams sit opposite one another in chairs and a balloon is thrown into the middle by an umpire. Each team member then tries to tap the balloon over the heads of the opposing team so that it falls to the ground behind their row of chairs. The balloon must be kept in the air. If it falls to the ground, the team who was due to hit it loses a point.

348 AUCTION

Any age from teenagers up — Any number — Indoors — Equipment: play money and assorted objects.

A fun game for a mixed party of teenagers or adults. Assorted objects are put up for auction and placed at one end of the room. An auctioneer is appointed, and each boy or girl becomes a buyer. The auctioneer tries to sell the objects to the highest bidder by pointing out all their good selling points, and the players try to shout him down by calling out comments or bad points. Each player starts with fifty matches or paper clips (Monopoly money is fine if you have it) and the person with the most objects at the end of the game wins.

349 BIRDS CAN FLY

Any age from 5 or 6 – Any number – Indoors – Equipment: none.

The players stand in a line, facing the leader. The leader calls out: "Birds can fly", and waves and flaps his arms about. All players must follow suit. Then the leader might call out: 'Bees can fly', 'Butterflies can fly'. Each time, the players flap their arms. Suddenly, however, the leader may announce: 'Pigs can fly', and wave his arms about. Any player who waves his arms is out . . . because he just wasn't listening. The game can continue with 'Tigers can growl' (in which everyone makes growling noises) or any other variation.

350 CHAIN TALKING

Any age from 10 or 11 – Any even number – Indoors – Equipment: none.

Choose two teams and let a judge give each a subject to talk about. The first member of one team talks about his subject as long as he can. Then the next team member takes over and so on until the whole team have finished. The judge, meanwhile, has kept score of the time, and then times the second team with their subject. The team who talk the longest win. (To make this game last longer and be more fun, the judge should be pretty lax about insisting on keeping to the original subject.)

351 CONVERSATIONS

Any age over 9 or 10 – 2 players at a time – Indoors – Equipment: none.

For two players at a time, or members of a team. Two players are secretly given three phrases which they must work into a perfectly logical conversation. Then the contestants engage in conversation, each trying to steer it to a subject in which he can use his phrases. First one to do so wins.

352 SALUJEE

Any age from 7 or 8 – Any number – Outdoors – Equipment: old knotted towel.

Salujee is played with a knotted towel by any number of players standing in a circle. 'It' stands in the middle and tries to catch the towel as the players throw it from one to another. When 'It' catches the towel, he changes places with the last person to hold it. Players may add to 'It's' general frustration by gently patting him with the knotted towel when his back is turned.

353 DRAMA CLASS

Any age from 6 or 7 – Any number – Indoors – Equipment: none.

Choose a judge to decide which player is the best actor or actress. He tells them to interpret an emotion such as rage, despair, hope, fear, misery, happiness, infatuation, etc. Each round is judged from purely facial expressions and the best one wins.

354 TIN TIME

Any age over 7 or 8 — Any number — Indoors — Equipment: Some unopened cans of food, a written list (see below) and a pencil for each player.

Crayon a number on the top of five, six or seven cans, take off the labels and write the same numbers on the back of them so you will know what you have got when the cans go back on the shelf. The players have to guess by feel, shaking and weight which can is which from the list of contents handed to them. The nearest correct guess wins a prize.

355 ALIBI

Teenagers or adults 2 teams of any number plus one judge — Indoors – Equipment: none.

Two teams and a judge are appointed. The first team is the prosecution and the second team the accused. The prosecution team accuses a member of the other team of some preposterous crime, and concocts a watertight prosecution case to ensure a conviction. The defence team have to put forward a defence, alibis and plausible explanations for all the facts put forward by the prosecution. Witnesses are called and give evidence. The judge's decision is final. If he wishes, the judge can dismiss the case and the two sides reverse rôles.

356 LETTER AUCTION

Any age from 9 or 10 — Up to 8 players — Indoors — Equipment: 50 matchsticks each, and alphabet cards.

Each player starts with fifty matchsticks and three cards from an

alphabet pack. Each player puts five matchsticks into the kitty and the dealer turns up the rest of the cards one at a time. Each player bids for the cards as they turn up — with the object of making the longest word he can. If no one bids for a card, it is automatically added to the next one as a bonus. Every three-letter word laid down gains two matchsticks from the kitty, every four-letter word gets three matchsticks and a five-letter word is worth four matchsticks. Six-letter words or over are worth six matchsticks. The first player to scoop the kitty or leave all his opponents without matchsticks wins the game.

357 NAMES

Any age from 9 or 10 — Up to 8 players — Indoors — Equipment: a pack of alphabet cards and a dictionary.

Before starting to play, the players decide whether to choose cities, animals, birds, flowers, etc. A pack of alphabet cards is laid face downwards and the first player takes one from the top. He then has to think of the longest word in the chosen group which begins with the letter on the card. For instance, if playing 'animals', the first player might turn up a 'B' and call out 'Bear'. Another player might pick up an 'R' and call 'Rhinoceros'. The 'Rhinoceros' would win all the cards on that round, if it were the longest word called. When the pack is exhausted, the player with most cards is the winner.

358 STEAL

Any age from 9 or 10 — Up to 8 players — Indoors — Equipment: a pack of alphabet cards.

Alphabet cards are dealt out to all the players, who have to make the longest word they can. Each player, however, may choose a card from someone else (without looking at the face of the card, of course). That person must part with it, but he then chooses a letter from the first player in return. The idea is to get rid of all unwanted cards. Opponents should watch each other carefully. If anyone pays special attention to a card, then it is probably a useful letter or one which he needs for a long word. The first player to make a complete word lays it down. If no one can put down a longer word, he has won.

359 ALPHABET CHEAT

Any age from 9 or 10 — Up to 8 players — Indoors — Equipment: a pack of alphabet cards.

It is possible to play a form of 'Cheat' with alphabet cards. The rules of the game are the same (*see Game 441*), except that a person is allowed one cheating move in every word. (He can either spell a word wrongly by one letter, or use a card which is different from what he says it is.) Instead of laying down the cards face up, they are placed face down, so that no one really knows whether the word is genuine or a cheat. Any player may accuse another of cheating. Then the player must turn up his word. If he was not cheating, he takes all the cards from his accuser. If he was cheating, the accuser wins the cards. Words score one point for every letter, and the player with the highest score wins.

360 RHYMES

Any age from 9 or 10 — Up to 8 players — Indoors — Equipment: a pack of alphabet cards.

Alphabet cards are dealt out to the players and the first one lays down a three-letter word. If any other players can lay down a rhyming word of three letters these cards go into the kitty. The first person to lay down a word that no one can rhyme scoops the kitty.

361 BLOCKING

Any age over 8 or 9 – 2 or 4 players – Indoors – Equipment: a set of dominoes.

All the dominoes are shuffled face downwards. Each player draws seven pieces, and any left over are left as stock and not used in this game. The person with the highest single domino lays down first. If it is a double, he gets an extra go. The next player puts down a domino with pips of the same number as those at either end of the pieces in play. If he cannot go, he has to pass and let the next player take his turn. The game ends when one player lays down his last domino or when nobody can make a move. The winner is the one with the lowest total of pips in his possession and he scores the total number of points held by all his opponents.

362 DRAWING

Any age over 8 or 9 – 2 or 4 players – Indoors – Equipment: a set of dominoes.

This is played in the same way as the Blocking game, except that if a player cannot go he must pick up from stock until he can. If more than two players are taking part, they start out with only five pieces instead of seven.

363 FIVES AND THREES

Any age over 8 or 9 – 2 or 4 players – Indoors – Equipment: a set of dominoes.

The object of this game is not to get rid of the dominoes but to make fives and threes or multiples of five and three. If a player puts down a 6–3, for instance, he has automatically scored three points, since he can claim three times three. If the next player were lucky enough to have the double six, he would place it down crosswise by the first piece and claim his four points for having made a total of twelve (or four times three). If a player cannot go because he cannot match a number at either end, he draws from stock until he can. When no players can go, the one with the lowest total of pips on his remaining pieces scores one extra point.

364 MATADOR

Any age over 8 or 9 – 2 or 4 players – Indoors – Equipment: a set of dominoes.

The object here is not to match dominoes but to make a total of seven. Thus if a 4–2 started the game, the next player would need either a three or a five on one of his pieces. There are four 'matadors' . . . the double blank, the 6–1, the 5–2 and the 4–3. These can be laid at any time even if the pips at either end do not add up to seven. When a player cannot go he draws from stock. First man out claims the total of points represented by all unplayed pieces.

365 HOP THE LEMONS

Any age – Any even number – Indoors or outdoors – Equipment: 2 lemons, 2 small egg cups.

The teams line up. Two lemons are balanced in small egg cups, the smaller the better. The teams have to hop without dropping the lemons to the finishing line and back to hand over to the next team member. If it drops they have to go back to the line they last left before starting again. No holding the lemon, only the base of the eggcup. The hopping motion makes this rather hard !

366 PENNIES ON THE PLATE

Any age from 6 or 7 – Any number – Indoors or outdoors – Equipment: an old plate and 6 pennies for each player.

A plate (preferably old and unwanted) is placed on the floor some eight feet from the competitors who try to toss half a dozen pennies on to it. The player who lands the most pennies on the plate wins.

367 PENNY ROLL

Any age from 8 or 9 – Any number – Indoors – Equipment: 2 books and a supply of pennies.

Two books are placed at one end of the room about two inches apart. Competitors bowl pennies along the floor from eight or ten feet away and try to roll the penny between the books. The one who gets the most pennies through the gap wins.

368 PENNY SLIDES

Any player from 8 or 9 – Any number – Indoors – Equipment: a 'target', and pennies for all players.

For this you need a large patch of smooth linoleum or polished floor. A quarter or a plastic disk is used as the target, and players clide pennies across the playing area aiming to get as near the target as possible. Other competitors try to knock their opponents' coins out of the way.

369 PENNY ON THE LINE

Any age from 6 or 7 – Any number – Indoors – Equipment: adhesive tape or string to mark a line, and pennies for all players.

From a distance of six or eight feet, players toss pennies and try to land them on the line. The first player to do so scoops up all the coins already played. The eventual winner ends up with a piggy-bank full of pennies.

370 PROPS

Any age from 9 or 10 – Any even number – Indoors – Equipment: paper bags, collections of oddments for each team.

Choose two teams and give each leader a paper bag containing a variety of odd things. The teams are given five minutes to concoct a little play introducing every one of the items in some way. The stranger the assortment of objects the better.

371 THIMBLE RACE

Any age over 8 or 9 – Teams of equal numbers – Indoors – Equipment: a drinking straw for each child plus 2 thimbles.

Each player is given an ordinary drinking straw, which is held in the mouth. The first player of each team has a thimble placed on the end of his straw by the leader. On the word 'GO' the thimble is passed down the line and back again from straw to straw.

372 NEWSPAPER JIGSAW

Any age from 8 or 9 – Any even number – Indoors – Equipment: 2 cut up pages of a newspaper.

Two pages are taken from the same newspaper and cut up so that each member of the team gets one piece. Then the teams must put the pieces together again properly. The paper should be cut in irregular shapes.

373 RHYTHM

Any age from 10 or 11 – Any number – Indoors – Equipment: none.

All players start hand-clapping to a regular beat. On the fourth beat, the first player says a word. Four beats later the player next to him must say a word which is associated in some way, such as 'cat', 'dog'. Each player takes a turn every four beats. Anyone who falters, breaks the rhythm or says an odd word is eliminated. When each player has had his turn, the words are spoken on every third beat, then on the second and finally on every beat. This soon eliminates just about everyone. Last person in is obviously the winner.

374 WORD HUNT

Any age from 7 or 8 – Any number – Indoors – Equipment: separate slips of paper, each bearing one letter of a six-letter word.

Give each player a number which he must remember. Then a six-letter word is chosen for each player and each letter of it written on a separate piece of paper – which also bears the person's number. The slips of paper are hidden all over the house (or room) and the players have to find their six pieces of paper, and re-assemble them into the right word. The first player to do this wins.

375 CAMOUFLAGE

Any age from 8 or 9 – Any number – Indoors – Equipment: familiar objects in an unfamiliar setting.

While the players go out of the room, 'It' hides a number of familiar objects in the room . . . but they must not be hidden right out of view. The trick is to place the objects near or against other things of

the same colour or texture. Players look for the objects and keep their discovery to themselves. After a while, each player is asked how many he picked out and the one giving the highest number is asked to prove his figures by picking up the articles.

376 APPLE RACE

Teenagers or adults – Teams of 4 – Indoors – Equipment: a plate, an apple and a knife for each team.

Choose teams of four. The leader of each is given an apple and a table knife. He has to peel the apple and pass it on to number two, who cuts it in two. Number three cuts the apple into quarters, and number four puts the pieces on the plate, runs to the front of the team, gives the plate to number one before returning to his place. The first team to finish wins the race.

377 CENTIPEDE RACE

Any age from 6 or 7 – Teams of 4 – Indoors or outdoors – Equipment: none.

Choose teams of four. Everyone gets down on hands and knees and the teams line up behind their leader. The second member grasps the leader by his ankles, and the player behind him grabs hold of his ankles – as does the last team member. Then the starting signal is given and the 'centipedes' must race across the room, turn round and return to the starting point without breaking the hand and ankle hold.

126

378 MINT RELAY

Teenagers or adults – Teams of even numbers – Indoors – Equipment: a cocktail stick for each player plus a mint with a hole for each team.

Two teams are given a cocktail stick each and a mint in which a hole has been cut. The leader balances the mint on his cocktail stick (held in his mouth) and passes it on to the next member who repeats the procedure. First team to pass the mint up and back down the line wins.

379 SHOE SCRAMBLE

Any age from 6 or 7 – Teams of even numbers – Indoors or outdoors – Equipment: children's own shoes.

Everyone takes off their shoes and throws them into a jumbled pile. Then players form into two teams and line up along a starting line. The first player of each team runs to the pile of shoes, sorts out his own pair and puts them on. Then he runs back to his team and the second player takes over. First team wearing footwear again wins. See drawing.

380 NIGHT OUT

Any age from 6 or 7 – Any number of pairs – Indoors – Equipment: none.

The subject is 'A Night Out'. Players in pairs take it in turns to perform a mime and the other players have to guess what they are doing . . . playing a flute, bowling, going to the cinema or whatever.

381 DITTO

Icebreaker – Any age over 6 or 7 – Any number – Indoors or outdoors – Equipment: none.

Players sit closely together in a circle. The first player turns to the person on his right and pats his head, squeezes his arm, tickles him or just makes a funny face. This player then does the same thing to his next-door-neighbour and so on round the circle until it comes back to the first player. The player to the right of the first leader then performs the next action. The object is to play with dead serious faces . . . anyone who laughs or giggles is out.

382 SILLY TILLIE

Any age over 9 or 10 – Any number – Indoors – Equipment: none.

This game can only be played once, because when the secret is out, it is finished. It starts quite impromptu when two people (who are in the know) suddenly announce: 'We are going to talk about Silly

Tillie. Anyone can join in.' One of these players will then say: 'Silly Tillie loves coffee but hates tea'.

The other player says : 'Silly Tillie likes bass but hates trout'.

First player could say : 'Silly Tillie loves bees but not honey'.

Eventually, another player will catch on and say something like : 'Silly Tillie wears wool but not silk'.

The point is that Silly Tillie likes ANYTHING that contains a double letter. Even her name is a clue. The last player to catch on ought to pay a forfeit for being so slow.

383 BOXING BOTTLE CAPS

Any age from 5 or 6 – Any number – Indoors – Equipment: an egg box with its top removed, and 6 bottle caps.

Place the egg box at one end of a table (against a wall if you can). Each player then takes turns standing at the other end of the table and tossing the bottle caps into the compartments of the egg box. Award six points for scores in the two centre compartments, three points for scores in the four other compartments. Highest score wins.

384 ODD ASSOCIATIONS

Any age over 9 or 10 – Any number – Indoors – Equipment: none.

One player thinks of a word – and then calls out an oblique or vague clue associated with it. The other players in turn ask him three questions and at the end someone must make a guess at the word. (For example : a player might call out 'Rat' when the word he was thinking of was 'belfry'. The association in this case is that rat rhymes with bat and bats live in belfries.)

385 CRAB AND MONKEY RELAY

Any age from 7 or 8 – 2 teams of equal numbers – Indoors or out-doors – Equipment: none.

Two teams line up and walk the course with both hands dragging on the floor or grass (monkey-style) and return on hands and knees backwards (crab-style). The first team 'home' wins.

386 DAFT DISCUS THROW

Any age from 8 or 9 – Any number – Indoors – Equipment: a paper bag for each player. (And remove small ornaments).

Give each player a paper bag to blow up. Then, holding the bag in the style of the classical Greek discus thrower he must hurl it as far as possible across the room. Just try to hurl a paper bag full of air in any one direction ! The game soon becomes hilarious.

387 SAUSAGE BALLOON TOSSING

Any age from 8 or 9 – Any number – Indoors – Equipment: sausage-shaped balloons.

For an amusing variation on the Highland Games, try tossing a blown-up sausage-shaped balloon. Booby prizes are in order for the shortest throw.

388 BAG BANG RELAY

Any age from 8 or 9 – Teams of equal numbers – Indoors or outdoors – Equipment: paper bags.

Each member of the teams is given a paper bag. On the starting signal, the leader of each team blows up his bag and bursts it by clapping with it between his hands. This is the signal for the next player to blow up his bag and do the same . . . and so on down the line.

389 BOAT RACE

Any age from 6 or 7 – Teams of equal numbers – Indoors or outdoors – Equipment: none.

Each team forms a 'boat' by every player kneeling with his hands resting on the shoulders of the player in front. Each team has a guide, who stands facing his boat and holding the hands of the first player. Both guides try to guide their boat team to victory across a short course by calling out movements in rhythm so that the 'boat' moves in unison. If a 'boat' breaks up, it is considered to have sunk.

390 TOFFEE APPLE

Teenagers or adults – Teams of equal numbers – Indoors – Equipment: 2 apples and some cocktail sticks.

Divide the players into teams. Each team member is then given a cocktail stick to hold in his mouth. The apple is passed by spearing the apple on the stick and passing it on.

391 VANITY

Adults – Any even number – Indoors – Equipment: a list of descriptions (see below), paper and a pencil for each player.

Write out imaginary descriptions of six men and six women and number them. The descriptions can read: tall, handsome, suave, fat, sleepy, pudgy, etc. Each player has to write down which description he thinks suits him best and gives this to the host. The players are then divided into two teams, and each team in turn has to guess which description each member of the other team has chosen for himself. A guess which is right first time scores three points, a second guess two points, and a third one point.

392 PLATE AND MARBLES RACE

Any age from 7 or 8 – 2 teams of even numbers – Indoors or outdoors – Equipment: a shallow plate and 4 marbles for each team.

Teams stand one behind the other in lines. The leaders are given a shallow plate with four marbles on it. They must pass the plate of marbles back down the line over their heads. When the plate reaches the end it is passed back under the players' legs. If any marbles drop off the plate, they must be replaced before continuing.

393 PEAS ON A KNIFE RACE

Any age from 7 or 8 – 2 teams of even numbers – Indoors – Equipment: 2 dried peas and a stick for each team.

Each team is given two dried peas and one flat wooden stick. Balancing the peas on the blade of the stick, each competitor in turn must cross the room and return safely. (**Note: If you have no flat wooden sticks, forget this game. Do NOT be tempted to play it using real knives**). See drawing.

394 TWO DOGS, ONE BONE

Any age from 6 or 7 – 2 teams of equal numbers – Indoors – Equipment: a ball or a duster.

A rubber ball, or even a duster is placed on the floor. Two teams sit in rows of chairs an equal distance from this 'bone'. Each team member is then given a number, starting from opposite ends, so that both Number Ones are at opposite ends of the rows. A leader then calls out any number, and the players with that number make a dash for the 'bone'. The player who seizes the 'bone' first scores a point for his team. When all the numbers have been called, the team with the most points wins.

395 COUNTER SPOOF

Any age over 7 or 8 – Any number, in pairs – Indoors – Equipment: an equal number of buttons for each player.

The two contestants conceal the buttons in their palms. Each player holds his hands behind his back while he sorts out the number of buttons he wishes to display. Hands must not be opened until both contestants have had a guess at the total. This is a variation of Finger Spoof.

396 THE WAITER'S RELAY

Any age over 6 or 7 – Any even number – Indoors – Equipment: a paper cup and plate for each player.

Form the players into two teams and give each person a paper plate. At the far end of the room place two even groups of paper cups. On

the word 'GO' Number One in each team runs forward, picks up a cup, puts it on the plate and, using *one hand* only, runs back to his team. Number Two takes the plate and cup from him, puts his own plate on top of the cup, runs forward, collects another cup, brings it back, and hands over to Number Three. This continues down the team until all the cups have been collected. Any person who drops his cups and plates has to take his turn again. First team home wins.

397 LIARS

Any age over 9 or 10 – 2 teams of 3–4 players – Indoors or outdoors – Equipment: none.

This is a very simple game. Two teams of three or four players each have to concoct a story based on fact – some local episode in which they were involved or something that happened at school. The story is true except for one tiny lie in it. The other team is allowed three guesses as to the lie. Three points are scored for a correct first guess, two for a second, and one for a third. The teams then change over and the liars become the guessers.

The addition of plenty of minute detail to the story makes the lie much more difficult to spot.

398 BALLOON PUMP

Any age from 7 or 8 – Teams of equal numbers – Indoors – Equipment: 2 bicycle pumps and 2 balloons.

For this game you need two bicycle pumps and two blown-up balloons. Players form into teams, the leaders take the pumps and blow their balloons across the room and back again. The second player repeats and so on, until one team has finished.

399 THE JIGSAW GAME

Any age over 6 or 7 – any number – Indoors – Equipment: a full-page colour picture or advertisement from a magazine for each player, cardboard, glue or paste, scissors, and an envelope or paper bag for each jigsaw.

This game needs a little preparation in advance, but should guarantee a short spell of peace after dinner. You will need for each player a full-page colour picture from a magazine. Paste this on to a piece of cardboard, and then cut it into smallish pieces to make a jigsaw puzzle. Shuffle the pieces around, and then put them into an envelope or paper bag. Each player is given an envelope or bag, which he opens on the word 'GO'. The first player to complete his jigsaw wins the game.

400 CHARLIE CHAPLIN RACE

Any age from 7 or 8 – Teams of equal numbers – Indoors (be careful !) or outdoors – Equipment: a balloon, walking stick and a cushion for each team.

This game *could* be the way that Charlie Chaplin practised his famous walk. Who knows? However, it is definitely one way in which to spread good humour. Played as a team relay, each player has to waddle across the room with a balloon held firmly between the knees, a soft cushion balanced on the head, and twirling a walking stick. If the cushion, stick or balloon is dropped, it must be picked up and put back into place before continuing.

401 WIVES CAN'T TELL

Adults — Any number of couples — Indoors — Equipment: a blindfold.

Each wife in turn is blindfolded, and puts one hand behind her back. The men in turn shake hands with the hand behind her back — without giving any sign which might help to identify them. The wife has to find her own husband — and only one guess is allowed. Then it's the turn of the husbands. The game is not as easy as it sounds — although rings may give clues about identity. The winners are the husband and wife who find their partners first time and/or in the shortest time.

402 NOT AT NIGHT

Adults — Any number of couples — Indoors — Equipment: a blindfold.

The players sit in a circle, and wives and husbands take it in turn to be blindfolded. While the other players pretend to snore, the blindfolded person has to move around, find his or her mate, and sit down on his or her lap. The other players make this more difficult by quietly changing places with each other as the game progresses. This game is a variation of Wives Can't Tell.

403 ODD OR EVEN

Any age from 5 or 6 — Any number — Indoors or outdoors — Equipment: 4 marbles or plastic disks for each.

A variation of Counter Spoof and suitable for younger children. Everyone is given four marbles or plastic disks. They sort any number of disks into their right hand and challenge other players to guess whether they are holding an odd or even number in their closed fist. A correct guess wins the disks, a wrong guess, and the guesser is out. One overall winner emerges at the end.

404 PAPER CATCH

Any age from 5 or 6 — Any number — Indoors — Equipment: sheets of thin paper.

Someone stands on a chair, holding several sheets of ordinary writing paper. One by one, he lets them float to the ground, having challenged other players to catch the sheets using their finger and thumb only. It's not quite as easy as it sounds.

405 MIRROR DRAWING

Any age from 7 or 8 — Any number — Indoors — Equipment: a large mirror, pencils and paper for each player.

Set up a mirror on a table and give players a sheet of paper and a

pencil. They are asked in turn to draw a simple object — such as a house, or an animal — while looking into the mirror. The results are amusing, for most people are surprised to realise their inability to draw even the simplest shape while concentrating on a mirror-image.

406 EGG IN A BOTTLE

Equipment: a hard-boiled egg (shelled) and an empty milk bottle.

Shell a hard-boiled egg and stand it on the open neck of an empty milk bottle. Tell your guests that you can get the egg into the bottle without damaging it. AND that you can do the trick without even touching the egg. Then go ahead and prove it. Take a match, light it, and drop it quickly into the milk bottle. Then, very quickly, push the sharp end of the egg into the neck of the bottle. The flame of the match burns away all the oxygen inside the bottle and creates a vacuum. The egg is sucked into the bottle automatically. See drawing.

407 EGG OUT OF THE BOTTLE

Equipment: the same egg, the same bottle.

Having performed this amazing feat, tell your guests that you can also get the egg out again without breaking the bottle. Hold the bottle upside down, so the egg falls into the neck. Now hold the bottle to your mouth and blow in hard. Remove the bottle from your lips and the pressure inside blows the egg out.

408 I OWN A GARAGE

Teenagers or adults – Any number – Indoors – Equipment: none.

This is a more sophisticated version of Market, and just as much fun. One player starts the game off by saying: 'I own a large garage and in it I keep a Ford car'. The second player must add something – such as: 'I own a large garage and in it I keep a Ford car and a Cadillac car'. The third player might say: 'I own a large garage and in it I keep a Ford car, and a Cadillac car and a can of gas'. Each player adds something, but has to repeat everything which had gone before. If they forget or get mixed up, they drop out.

409 INSIDE OUT

Any age from 7 or 8 – Any number – Indoors or outdoors – Equipment: none.

Players must lie face down on the floor, draw their legs up behind them and hold their feet with their hands. Now, without letting go, they must wriggle over on to their backs. It is not as easy as it sounds, and the contortions are very funny to watch.

410 MUSICAL HATS

Any age from 5 or 6 – Any number – Indoors – Equipment: party hats and music.

A variation on the game of Musical Chairs. Players sit in a circle and while music plays they pass party hats around. There is one fewer hat than players. When the music stops everyone with a hat puts it on. The poor player left without a hat drops out of the game, taking one hat with him.

411 DROP AND GUESS

Any age from 6 or 7 – Any number – Indoors – Equipment: a collection of small, different objects.

Players sit with their backs to the leader, who drops any number of small articles on to a table from a height of about six inches. Players must guess what article was dropped from the sound it makes. Some suggestions for objects to be dropped: coins, buttons, a thimble, boxes of matches, paper clips.

412 ALLITERATION

Any age from 7 or 8 – Any number – Indoors – Equipment: none.

Players take turns to make three-word phrases that all start with the same letter. Start with one, then two, and so on.
   Examples: One Odious Onion, Two Tasty Tomatoes, Three Thirsty Thrushes, Four Fat Fish, Five Frantic Frenchmen, Six Sizzling Sausages, Seven Succulent Saveloys, Eight Energetic Elephants, Nine Noisy Nightingales, Ten Twisting Tadpoles.

413 CROWS AND CRANES

Any age over 7 or 8 – Any even number – Indoors – Equipment: none.

Choose a team of Crows and a team of Cranes. Teams face one another and an umpire stands ready. He starts by saying 'Crrrrr . . .' so that neither team is sure whether he will call 'Crows' or 'Cranes'. As the tension increases, the umpire calls out 'Crows' or 'Cranes', and that team immediately race for the wall behind them, touch it and return to reform their line. The opposing team must catch players before they reach the wall. If they do, the caught player becomes a member of the opposite team. The winning team is the one that finally has the most players.

414 TIE THE TIE

Icebreaker — Teenager or adults — Even numbers of boys and girls — Indoors — Equipment: none.

Each boy undoes his tie, and his female partner then has to tie it into a bow tie *from behind*. All boys should choose shorter girls, if possible, as partners. Best bow tie in 15 seconds wins.

415 BALLOON DANCE

Icebreaker – Any age from 6 or 7 – Pairs of boys and girls – Indoors – Equipment: a balloon for each pair.

Choose boy and girl pairs and give each pair an inflated balloon. They must hold the balloon between their two noses. Not only that, they must join hands and dance round to a clapping rhythm supplied by players who are not taking part. As the rhythm gets faster and faster, the couples who drop their balloon drop out of the game.

416 SCRATCH-CAT

Any age from 5 or 6 – Any number – Indoors – Equipment: none.

'Scratch-cat' walks around on the floor on hands and knees, while the other players dance around him. They try to stroke the cat, and the cat swipes out with his paw and tries to scratch his tormentors. If 'Scratch-cat' manages to touch a player, he gets down on all fours and becomes a cat as well.

417 SINGING BLINDMAN

Any age from 5 or 6 – Any number – Indoors – Equipment: 1 thimble.

All the players leave the room while someone hides a thimble in a spot which is reasonably visible. The players come in and look round for the thimble – but if they see it, they must not betray its where-abouts to any player. They just sit down and start to sing: 'Three Blind Mice'. The last person to find the thimble is called the 'Blind-man' . . . but has the privilege of hiding the thimble next time.

418 ROLL IN THE BOWL

Any age from 9 or 10 – 2 teams of equal numbers – Indoors – Equip-ment: a fruit bowl and a marble for each team.

Each team is given a fruit bowl containing a marble. The first player starts the marble rolling round the rim of the bowl and then passes it on to the next player. The bowl must be passed right down the line with the marble always on the move. If the marble flies out of the bowl the player must retrieve it before passing on the bowl.

419 BALLOON WALK

Any age over 7 or 8 – Any number – Indoors or outdoors – Equipment: a balloon for each player.

Line the players up in a row, give each a balloon and ask him to hold it between his knees. On the word 'GO' the players must begin to walk towards the opposite end of the room. The person who can walk farthest without dropping his balloon wins.

420 BROKEN BOTTLES

Any age over 6 or 7 – Any number – Outdoors – Equipment: a small ball.

Players stand in a large circle and throw a small ball to each other. If anyone drops the ball, he has 'broken a bottle' and must pay the penalty. The first penalty – place the left hand behind the back. The second penalty – go down on one knee. The third penalty – go down on both knees. The next time he drops a ball the player is out.

421 HAND AND BUCKET CRICKET

Any age over 7 or 8 – Any number – Outdoors – Equipment: 2 plastic buckets and a small ball.

All you need is a 'cricket pitch'. The 'wickets' are two plastic buckets. The pitcher tosses a soft ball, aiming to get it into the bucket. The batter stands in front of his bucket and defends it with the flat of his hand only. But if the pitcher gets the ball into one of the buckets, the batter is out.

422 WITCH-HUNT

Any age from 10 or 11 – Any number (but not for the nervous) – Indoors – Equipment: none.

This is played all over the house with the lights turned out. The player chosen to be the witch runs off to hide. When the lights go out, the rest of the players go to find her. They call out: 'Are you there, witch?' and the witch gives a spooky cackle . . . then runs off to hide somewhere else. If anyone catches the witch, they shout out, the lights are turned on and the finder becomes the next witch.

423 SOUND BROADCAST

Any age from 9 or 10 – Any number – Indoors – Equipment: none.

A leader starts to tell a story to the other players. The story should contain as many sounds and noises as possible. As the leader mentions each noise, he points to one of the players who has to give his impression of the sound. The story can go on for as long as the leader likes.

A typical story might start: 'It was a stormy night and the wind was whistling. In the trees an owl hooted and a wolf howled. Horses galloped through the forest. Suddenly there was a clap of thunder and the rain splashed against the trees...

424 BUZZ, PHIZZ AND SPLOT

Any age from 11 or 12 – Any numbers – Indoors – Equipment: none.

Players must count quickly from one to twenty ... but number three is called 'Splot', number six is called 'Phizz' and number twelve is called 'Buzz'.

Everyone is amused as others get terribly mixed up trying to change from numbers to silly words. To make things even more complicated, try the following:

3	= Splot	12	= Buzz
6	= Phizz	15	= Flop
8	= Pinge	17	= Plip
10	= Flange	20	= Grooby

425 WINKING

Icebreaker – Any age from 11 or 12 – Equal number of boys and girls – Indoors – Equipment: none.

Girls sit on a circle of chairs, facing inwards. One chair is left empty. Boys stand behind ALL chairs, with their hands behind their backs, and the one who has no girl in his chair must attract one by winking at her. As soon as a girl is winked at, she jumps up and runs for the empty chair ... and the boy standing behind her can stop her by clapping his hands on her shoulders, but he must not leave his spot. The person doing the winking can resort to low trickery by staring in one direction, then changing and winking at a girl somewhere else. As the girls move around, each boy with the empty chair does the winking.

426 CITY WALLS

Any age over 5 or 6 – Any number, in 4 or 5 teams – Outdoors – Equipment: none.

Players form into four or five teams and each team leader appoints two players to be the 'City Gates'. These 'Gates' join hands above their heads to form an arch and stand in a line side by side. Other players dance round them and when the leader shouts 'ATTACK' all the players rush to pass through their own city gates and line up behind them. The last line to reform itself drops out. The game goes on until one city is victorious.

427 CORNY

Any age over 9 or 10 – Any even number – Indoors or outdoors – Equipment: none.

Each member of a team must tell a joke but miss the punch line. The other team must guess the missing line (or point) to score a mark. Then it is their turn. This is not all that difficult, as most people dry up and can't remember anything better than 'Why did the chicken cross the road?' or 'Who was that lady?' These jokes can carry a penalty if you like, but penalty jokes must be written down beforehand to avoid arguments

428 SAUSAGES AND BOLONEY

Any age from 7 or 8 – Any number – Indoors – Equipment: a well-known book suitable to the age group.

Players take turns to read aloud from a well-known book, but for every word that begins with an 's' the word 'sausages' is substituted. Every word starting with a 'b' becomes 'Boloney'. Nobody must laugh . . . upon penalty of expulsion!

429 PAT BALL

Any age over 9 or 10 – Any number – Outdoors – Equipment: 1 rubber ball.

Players stand in a circle. The first player bounces an ordinary rubber ball on the ground, and pats it with the palm of his hand for one more bounce. Then, in a clockwise direction, each player has to bounce the ball twice without letting it stop. The first player to miss drops out. Anyone who bounces the ball in the wrong direction is out as well.

430 DARTS FOOTBALL

For adults – Any even number – Indoors – Equipment: a darts board and darts.

This is played with two teams. Each player aims for the bull, and if he hits it he scores a goal for his team and takes the 'ball' out of play. The opposing team must then score a double to regain possession of the 'ball' before they can start aiming for the goal (or bullseye) once again.

431 DARTS CRICKET

For adults – Any even number – Indoors – Equipment: a darts board and darts.

Each team takes turns to 'bat' and 'bowl'. The batting side aims for doubles, scoring that number of runs when successful. The bowling side aims for the bullseye, and if they hit one then the batting side have lost a wicket. Play the game for an agreed number of wickets. Either team can declare at any time.

432 ANKLE SHOW

Any age from 12 or 13 – Any number – Indoors – Equipment: an old sheet.

This guessing game is good for a laugh. A large screen is improvised from an old sheet and a chair is placed behind it. The girls go behind the screen and take off their shoes. Then, one at a time, the girls sit on the chair and poke their feet and ankles underneath the sheet. The boys have to guess who the ankles belong to. Then the boys take their turn behind the screen, with the girls guessing which ankles belong to which boy. See drawing.

433 TWIRL THE SAUCER

Any age over 4 – Any even number – Indoors – Equipment: some old saucers, some tape to mark the finishing line.

This works best on a carpeted floor. Team members line up for a relay, according to numbers, and have to get their saucer to the finishing line for their partner to return it. The saucer may only be moved by twirling it while it is lying flat, with one finger only going round the raised edge. The most comfortable position for the player is on hands and knees. Pushing the finger round and round makes it zig-zag and difficult to control. No pushing or bowling is allowed – the saucer must be flat, and the right way up.

434 SHOVE HA'PENNY DARTS

For adults – Any number – Indoors – Equipment: a darts board and darts.

Each player throws three darts in turn, aiming to place all three in each segment from one to nine. A double scores two points and a treble three. If a player scores more than he needs in any segment, the extra is marked down to the next player who requires it — but the winning shot must be scored, and not received as a gift from another player. Sections may be filled in any order.

435 HIGHEST SCORE

For adults — Any number — Indoors — Equipment: a darts board and darts.

Each player throws three darts at the board, aiming for the highest score with just the three darts. The game is played for any number of rounds.

436 LOWEST SCORE

For adults — Any number — Indoors — Equipment: a darts board and darts.

Each player throws in turn, trying to score the lowest possible number. Darts off the board count twenty.

437 SHORT-THROW BULLSEYE

For adults — Any number — Indoors — Equipment: a darts board and darts.

Each player has three darts and stands four feet from the dartboard. He has to score a bullseye with each dart, having several goes in turn. The one who scores the greatest number of bulls is the winner.

438 TARGET SHOOT

For adults — Any number — Indoors — Equipment: a darts board and darts.

Each player has three darts. He has to score an exact total of thirty. The first person to do this wins. Darts off the board count for nothing.

439 HIT OR MISS

For adults — Any number — Indoors — Equipment: a darts board, darts, a pencil, a one-inch square of card for each guest, drawing-pins.

Before the party begins, write on each card either the name of the prize which the card-owner wins, or the forfeit he must pay, and then pin the cards, blank side uppermost, on to the dart board. According to which card he hits, each guest will either collect his prize or pay his forfeit.

440 SNAP

Any age from 6 or 7 — Up to 10 players — Indoors — Equipment: a pack of cards.

The pack is dealt out between the players. Each throws down a card in turn. When two cards of the same denomination go down consecutively, the first player to shout: 'Snap' wins all the pile. The winner is the one who has snapped up most cards.

441 CHEAT

Teenagers – Up to 10 players – Indoors – Equipment: pack of cards.

The more you cheat, the more likely you are to win this game . . . but you mustn't be caught out! The entire pack is dealt out to the players. The player to the left of the dealer lays face down one, two, three or four cards and announces what they are. He might, for instance, lay down four cards and say that they are four aces. Or he might lay down two cards and say they are two queens. Each player in turn lays down – and it is not important what he actually puts down, but what he *says* he puts down. Any time, any player may shout: 'Cheat', if he thinks the last player has been lying. The challenged player must then turn his cards over. If what he said was true, the challenging player must pick up all the cards on the table. If, however, the challenged player *was* cheating, then *he* must pick up all the cards. The object of the game is to get rid of all your cards first. Any cheating of any kind that goes undetected until the next player has laid his cards is permissible.

442 PELMANISM

For all the family, and guests over 6 or 7 – Any number up to 10 – Indoors – Equipment: a pack of cards.

The entire pack is spread out face down on the table and players take it in turns to look at any two cards, showing them to other players. If the chosen cards are of the same value, then the player keeps them.

When all the cards have been picked up, the player with the most pairs is the winner. Be warned — the youngest children always seem to win this.

443 NEWMARKET

Adults — For 6-8 players — Indoors — Equipment: a pack of cards and 10 plastic disks (or matchsticks) for each player.

Each player is given ten plastic disks. Before each game, one of these disks is placed into a central pool and goes to the winner.

The four aces are taken out of the pack and placed face up on the table. The pack is shuffled, and dealt to the players. The dealer deals one lot for himself and a spare, or 'dummy' set by the side of them. After looking at his own hand, he may discard it and choose the dummy if he wants to. If he is happy with his hand, he offers the dummy for sale, and any player may bid for it.

Each player now looks at his hand and lays another disk on any one of the four aces. Play starts with the person on the left of the dealer, who must lay his lowest red card (say the three of hearts). Now anyone who has the four of hearts must lay that . . . and so on. If a break in play occurs because the necessary card is in the dummy, then the last player lays down his lowest black. When a player lays down a king, he scoops the disks on the relevant ace. The first person to lay down all his cards wins the pool.

444 LIFTING AN ICE CUBE

Equipment: cup of water, ice cube, a small amount of salt, and a 6-inch piece of thread.

Place an ice cube in a cup of cold water, and challenge your guests to lift the ice out of the water using only a six-inch piece of thread. Most people will try to loop the thread round the ice cube, without success. When everyone has had a turn, show them how it is done. Dip the thread in the water until it is thoroughly wet. Then lay the thread across the top of the ice cube and sprinkle it well with salt. Leave for a few moments, and you will soon be able to lift out the ice cube on the end of the thread. See drawing.

445 OLD MAID

Any age over 12 or 13 — About 6–8 players — Indoors — Equipment: a pack of cards.

From the pack of cards, one queen is removed and the rest of the cards dealt out. Each player inspects his hand and lays down any pairs he has. If a player has three cards the same, he can only put down two of them, but if he has four the same, he puts them down as two pairs. Then the dealer offers his cards to the second player, holding them fanned out and face down. The second player chooses any card from the dealer's hand . . . and if he is lucky, pairs it with one of his own to place down. Then the second player offers his cards to the next player and so on. This continues until all the cards are down on the table in pairs . . . except for one player who will be holding the odd queen. This player is the 'Old Maid'. No one game has a winner. Play it for several rounds (at least twice for every player) and whoever has been 'Old Maid' the fewest times wins.

446 FARMYARDS

Any age over 11 or 12 – For 4 players – Indoors – Equipment: a pack of cards.

One pack of cards is needed for each four players. These are dealt out and each player places them in a neat pile by his side. Each player is then given the name of a farmyard animal – pig, cow, dog, etc., – and the first player lifts his first card from his pile and lays it face up on the table, next to his pile of cards. Each player does this, until a card goes down that matches any card showing on the table. That player must then make the farmyard noise of *the player whose card he matches* – if a cow turned up a two and he saw that a duck already had a two, the duck would moo and the cow would quack. Whoever first succeeds in imitating the correct noise wins all the cards showing. First person to collect all the cards is the winner.

447 DONKEY

Any age over 12 or 13 – Up to 13 players – Indoors – Equipment: a pack of cards.

This is an ideal game for larger groups, since each player has only four cards. If thirteen players take part, this is ideal. If twelve take part, then four cards of the same kind must be removed from the pack. If eleven take part, two sets of four matching cards must be removed . . . and so on.

When the dealer says: 'GO' each player takes a card from his hand and passes it to the player on his left. This goes on silently and continuously, with each player trying to assemble four matching cards and pass on the cards he does not want. As a player gains four of a kind, he puts them down on the table and that round is over. All the other players are now given the letter 'D' and a new game is played. The second time round, a player who loses gets the letter 'O', then 'N', 'K', 'E', and finally 'Y'. He is then a 'Donkey', and drops out of the game. As a player drops out, four matching cards are removed from the pack. When only two players are left, the first one to slap down his four cards is the winner.

448 UNDERSTUDY

Any age over 8 or 9 – Any number – Indoors or outdoors – Equipment: 5 tokens or counters for each player.

Each person in the room is given five counters and told he has to perform in some way – sing a song, recite a poem, tell a tale. The joke is that, having announced the specific poem or song he wishes to do, it has to be done by the person seated on his left. If that person does not know it he has to give one of his counters to the person who nominated the performance. A player may at any time challenge the nominator to perform the piece himself. If he fails he is out of the game. If he succeeds, the challenger hands over two of his counters. After each performance the performer nominates the next piece. The winner is the one with most counters at the end of the time allowed for the game.

449 BALLOON TAG

Any age from 5 or 6 – Any number – Outdoors – Equipment: 1 balloon (and spares, just to be safe.)

'It' is given an inflated balloon, which he throws in the air. At this point, all the other players run around, because they must avoid 'It's' deadly touch while the balloon is in the air. If caught, a player becomes the next 'It'. When the balloon touches the ground, everyone is safe until 'It' throws it up again.

450 SAFE SPOT TAG

Any age from 6 or 7 – Any number – Outdoors – Equipment: 1 large ball, and chalk to mark out a safe spot.

A game similar to Balloon Tag is played with a large ball. A safe spot is marked out on the ground and 'It' kicks the ball out of this spot and tries to catch other players. They can kick the ball, and if they kick it within the safe circle, 'It' cannot touch them. 'It' has to keep his eye on the ball at the same time as trying to catch players.

451 HADRIAN'S WALL

Any age from 6 or 7 – Any even number – Indoors – Equipment: none except markers.

Two teams, the Scots and the English, retire to opposite walls of the room. In the middle of the room, a no-man's land area about four feet wide is marked out and each team places a border guard there. Each team must try to cross into their opponent's territory, but the guards can catch any player in the central area. Guards cannot move out of their area. Caught players must pay a forfeit before leaving the game.

452 INDIAN WRESTLE

Any age from 7 or 8 – Any number in pairs – Indoors or outdoors – Equipment: none.

The contestants stand side by side, facing opposite ways, and place their right feet together. They grasp right hands and by pulling or pushing, each tries to force the other to move his right foot.

453 THE REFLEX GAME

Any age over 7 or 8 – Any number – Indoors – Equipment: a radio or record-player.

All the players sit down, while the host operates the radio or record-player, with his back to the players. The idea is that the players must try to guess when the music is going to stop – so the last person to get up before the music stops wins 1 point, while anyone still sitting loses a point. The host should try to fool the players by making exaggerated movements with his arms before he actually stops the music. The winner is the first person to score 5 points.

454 THE COUNTING GAME

Any age – Any number – Indoors – Equipment: none.

Each player in turn has to count aloud for as long as he can while being heckled or distracted by the others. The person who can keep going longest without hesitating or laughing wins.

455 POACHER AND KEEPER

Any age from 7 or 8 – Any number – Outdoors – Equipment: none.

Players form a circle around a cushion, and hold hands. One is (secretly) appointed 'Gamekeeper', and another plays the 'Poacher'. The poacher tries to get at the cushion in the ring. He may cross through any pair of linked arms, but must leave the same way. Only the gamekeeper may arrest him, but not until he has the cushion. The poacher has a difficult life, since he doesn't know who he is trying to avoid. When caught, the poacher becomes the gamekeeper.

456 CATCH THE RABBIT

Any age from 7 or 8 – 2 teams of equal numbers – Indoors or outdoors – Equipment: 1 small cushion.

Two teams line up in the centre of the playing area. Place a small cushion at one end. This is the 'rabbit'. On 'GO', the two team leaders race for the rabbit, the lucky one scoops it up, races back with it to the other end of the room and puts it on the ground. As he drops it, he calls: 'Rabbit' – and the Number Twos of each team race for the cushion and return it to its original position. . . and so on. Players who catch the rabbit line up behind their original team. The unlucky ones drop out. First team to dismiss the opposition wins.

457 CHINESE GET-UP

Any age over 5 or 6 – Any number in pairs – Indoors or outdoors – Equipment: none.

Players are sorted into pairs, who sit back to back on the ground with their arms folded across their chest. On the starting signal, each pair must try to stand up . . . but without uncrossing their arms. The only way to do this is for the partners to press their backs together until they can struggle to a standing position. First pair up wins.

458 GIDDY STICK

Any age from 7 or 8 – 2 teams of equal numbers – Outdoors – Equipment: 2 walking sticks.

Choose two teams and give each leader a walking stick. The leaders stand about eight–ten feet in front of their teams and hold the stick upright against the ground at arm's length. Team members race up to their leaders, grasp the stick and run round it three times, ducking under the leader's arm. After the third circuit they run back to their team and set off the next player. The first team to finish will be the giddy winners.

459 HEAD THROUGH A POSTCARD

Equipment: postcards and scissors.

Tell your guests that you can cut a hole in an ordinary post card big enough to put your head through No one will believe you. Take a few postcards, hand them out to guests and give them a pair of scissors, just to let them prove how impossible it is. Then take a postcard and scissors yourself and prove that the stunt can be done easily.

  First, cut slits in the card straight along the middle, stopping about

½″ from either end. Now cut other slits as in the diagram about ½″ apart and ending about ½″ from the edges. Then pull the postcard gently and fold back all the joints in alternate directions until you have a necklace which easily goes over your head.

460 SLAP JACK

Any age over 11 or 12 – For 4–5 players – Indoors – Equipment: a pack of cards.

One pack of cards is needed for every four or five players. These are dealt out and each player stacks them in a neat pile. Each player places his right elbow on the table so that he can slap the centre of the table when he wants to. Starting with the player next to the dealer, each player takes a card from his pile with his left hand and places it face upwards in the centre of the table. Whenever a Jack appears, every player tries to slap his hand down as quickly as possible. The player whose hand is first down scoops up all the cards. First player to win all the cards ends the game.

461 DANCE POP

Teenagers or adults – Equal numbers of men and girls – Indoors – Equipment: a balloon for each couple, music.

Couples start dancing back to back with their arms linked and with a balloon between their backs. While still dancing they have to turn slowly round so that they finish up dancing face to face with the balloon between them at the front. They must not touch the balloon with their hands and it must not fall to the ground – if it does, they have to start again. It can drop as low as the ankle, but has to be worked up again to chest level. First to finish wins.

462 BACKWARDS SPELLING BEE

Any age from 9 or 10 – Any number – Indoors – Equipment: none.

Leader calls out fairly simple words to each player in turn, who must spell it *backwards* in five or ten seconds. As players make mistakes they drop out of the game.

463 ODD EGG

Equipment: 1 fresh egg, one hard-boiled egg.

One trick you can play with eggs is to prove that you can always pick a fresh egg from a hardboiled one. The secret is simple. Take a fresh egg and one that has been hardboiled and give them a quick spin. The fresh egg will not spin nearly as easily as the hardboiled one.

464 HOLY SMOKE

For adults — Any number — Indoors — Equipment: a drinking glass, a paper napkin, and a dime.

Wet the rim of the glass and place the napkin over it, holding it taut so that the moisture on the rim soaks through. Then carefully tear away the surplus paper, so that you are left with a glass completely covered at the top with a circle of paper. Place a dime in the middle of the circle. Now each player in turn takes a lighted cigarette and just touches the circle of paper. This must be done very gently, but the paper must be seen to smolder. The amazing thing is how long it takes until the coin finally drops into the glass. When this eventually happens, the last person to have touched the paper with his cigarette has to pay a forfeit.

465 THE DEATH OF THE SQUIRE

Equipment: none.

Tell your guests the following story:

   Not so long ago, in a small village, a local Squire went with his wife to the church. During the sermon, the Squire nodded off and started dreaming. He dreamed that he was in France at the time of the Revolution and that he had been condemned to death on the guillotine. He dreamed that his neck was on the block, and the blade of the guillotine raised higher and higher. Then it started to fall. At this point, the Squire's wife noticed that he was asleep and tapped him smartly on the back of the neck with her fan. The shock was so great — in view of what the Squire was dreaming — that he died of fright.

   Now ask your guests whether the story is true or false. If they say it is false, ask them to prove it.

150

The way to prove the falsehood is simple : If the Squire died without waking up, no one could possibly know what he was dreaming about.

466 THE TWO INDIANS

Equipment: none.

For a quick piece of trickery, try this one on your guests :

There were two Indians who met after a long parting. One Indian was very old and the other Indian was very young. The young Indian was the old Indian's son, but the old Indian was not the young Indian's father. How can this contradiction be explained ?

...It's easy : the old Indian was the young Indian's *mother.*

467 MISSIONARIES AND CANNIBALS

Equipment: 3 pennies, 3 dimes, and a cigarette pack.

On one edge of a table, lay three pennies, three dimes, and a cigarette pack.

Tell the guests the following story:

There are three missionaries (the dimes) with a party of three cannibals (the pennies). They have come to a river (the table) and the only boat available (the cigarette pack) will carry only two people. Although all the missionaries could row the boat, only one cannibal (the chief) was able to do so. The problem is to get all the missionaries and all the cannibals across to the other side of the river ... but the important thing is that there can never be more cannibals than missionaries left alone on either side of the river. Give your guests a few minutes to puzzle this one over before showing them the solution.

How it is done: The cannibal chief rows across with one of his mates and returns for a second cannibal. The chief rows him across and returns. The two missionaries now take the boat over to the other side. One stays behind with one cannibal and the other missionary rows back with the other cannibal. Now a missionary rows across with the cannibal chief and brings back a cannibal. The two missionaries now row across and the cannibal chief returns in the boat to pick up his two mates in two trips. It takes thirteen trips in all.

468 HOW OLD ARE YOU DADDY?

Equipment: pencils and paper.

A little girl asked her father ; 'How old are you, Daddy?' The father answered her with a little rhyme :

'I was twice as old as you are
On the day that you were born ;
You will be as old as I was then
When fourteen years are gone.'

Ask your guests to puzzle out the age of the father. Give pencils and paper if needed, but no slide-rules.

Solution: The father is saying that he was twice as old as his daughter when she was born and that she will be the same age in fourteen years. So fourteen must be the key. Her father was twice that age (twenty-eight) when she was born fourteen years ago, so he must now be forty-two.

469 THE MAGNETIC PENCIL

Equipment: a pencil.

Hold up an ordinary pencil and tell your guests that you have enough magnetism in your body to make it defy gravity. Rub it a few times on your coat and then place it across your fingers on the upturned palm. Then, after touching it with the index finger of your other hand to adjust its position, you raise your hand in the air, palm towards yourself . . . and the pencil miraculously stays there.

The trick is simple: When you pretended to adjust the position, you clipped the pencil in position by placing your finger over it, and gripped your wrist with the other fingers and thumb to support the hand holding the pencil while you made this adjustment. Since your guests are not expecting trickery, none will notice that you are gripping your wrist with a thumb and only three fingers.

470 THE AMOEBA PUZZLE

Equipment: none.

Amoeba, as we learn at school, are simple, one-celled animals that reproduce by splitting themselves in half — or, to give it its scientific name, by binary fission.

Now for the problem. Tell your guests that a single amoeba is placed in an empty jar. This amoeba is as regular as clockwork and divides into two every minute on the dot. Each of the halves divide into others and so on, so that in half an hour, there are exactly 1,073,741,284 amoebæ in the jar.

The problem is this: If we had started with TWO amoebæ, how long would it have taken to produce exactly the same number?

To puzzle your guests futher, tell them that the time to solve the problem is ten seconds.

Solution: The answer will probably be a great surprise to everyone. It would take twenty-nine minutes (or just one minute less) to produce the same number. The reason for this, of course, is that during the first minute, the single amoeba was itself becoming two.

471 THE BOOKWORM

Equipment: none.

One day a professor went to his bookshelves and found that a bookworm had eaten his way from the first page of Volume One to the last page of Volume Three of a set of encyclopaedias. Each book was exactly $2\frac{1}{2}$" thick including the covers, which were each $\frac{1}{8}$" thick.

How far had the bookworm travelled? Your guests answers will be way out!

Solution: The worm had travelled only 2¾″. He only went through page one and the cover of Volume One, through 2½″ of Volume Two and through the cover of Volume Three.

472 TICK-TACK-TOE

Any age from 5 upward — Any numbers in pairs — Indoors — Equipment: pencils and paper.

Draw a double cross, like two railway lines crossing one another, and take it in turns to mark an 'X' or an 'O' in any square. First player to get three of his symbols in a straight line (up, across or diagonally) wins.

473 TOE-TACK-TICK

Age over 8 or 9 — Any number in pairs — Indoors — Equipment: a sheet of paper for each couple, a pencil for each player.

The title really explains the game — which is tick-tack-toe in reverse. Any player with a complete line of noughts or crosses *loses* the game, and is out. Play this on an elimination basis until you find the eventual winner.

474 BATTLESHIPS

Any age from 9 or 10 — 2 players at a time — Indoors — Equipment: pencils and paper.

Draw twelve rows of twelve lines, horizontally and vertically, on two sheets of paper, so that there are 144 squares on each. The squares along the top are numbered from one to twelve, and the squares running vertically are marked A to L. Thus any particular square has a reference . . . A7, G3, H9, etc. Each player then draws his 'Battleship Fleet' consisting of: 1 Aircraft carrier (5 blacked squares in a straight line) ; 1 Battleship (4 diagonal squares) ; 2 Cruisers (3 squares in a line) ; 3 Destroyers (2 squares) ; and 3 Submarines (1 square). No squares may be shared.

When both players have drawn their fleets, they take turns to 'shoot' at each other, by calling out a square reference. The opponent says 'Splash' if the shot is a miss, or 'Hit' if the square called has one of his ships on it. First to sink all the other's 'ships' wins.

475 PIGGIES

Any age from 6 or 7 — Any number – Indoors — Equipment: pencils and paper, and blindfolds.

A variation on The Donkey's Tail, in this game each player is given a sheet of paper and a pencil and tries to draw a pig while blindfolded. The results are passed around and the most accurate or amusing wins.

476 NUMBERED CHAIRS

Teenagers or adults — Any number — Indoors — Equipment: a chair for each player.

The chairs are placed in a line and each one is allotted a number, which stays constant throughout the game. The players sit down, and the game is started by the player in chair number one calling out the number of another chair — say, chair seven. The player sitting in chair seven must immediately call another number — say, number three. The player in chair three must call yet another number, and so on. As soon as someone fails to respond when his chair number is called, or answers out of turn, he must move to the chair at the end of the line, and all the other players move up one. As the numbering of the chairs remains unaltered throughout, each player must quickly try to memorise his new chair number each time he has to move up. This can be more difficult than it would appear — as the resulting confusion will show !

477 FEEL THE PAIRS

Adults — Any number — Indoors — Equipment: an assortment of small objects, a blindfold.

Each player is blindfolded, and has to identify the objects handed to him by touch alone. The trick is to collect together pairs of items which are similar in shape, texture and size — rubber eraser and a toffee candy, for example. You can have fun, if you like, with peeled tomatoes, peeled grapes and the like.

478 PARTY HOOP-LA

Any age over 6 or 7 — Any number — Indoors — Equipment: 6 paper cups and 6 or more paper covers from 45 r.p.m. records.

Stand the cups in a row upside down at the end of the room. Each player stands about eight feet away and tries to throw the record covers over the paper cups. The player with the highest score wins. If you haven't enough record covers, pieces of cardboard with a hole cut in the middle will do just as well.

479 WHAT'S MISSING ?

Any age over 9 or 10 — Any number — Indoors — Equipment: 20 or so small everyday articles, a tablecloth, and pencils and paper for each player.

Pile all the items (a pencil sharpener, a bottle top, a lipstick, some book matches, etc.) on a table and cover them with the tablecloth. Gather all the players round the table and explain that they will have one minute in which to study the pile of articles. Remove the cloth and, when the time is up, replace it again. Now slip your hand beneath the cloth and remove one item, taking care that it is not seen by the players. Remove the cloth once more and ask the players to write down which item has been removed. Repeat the procedure ten times, The player with the most accurate list of missing items wins.

480 GUESS THE SINGER – GUESS THE SONG

Teenagers or adults – Any number – Indoors – Equipment: a record-player and some records.

This is a good way to get the conversation going among the guests. Simply play a variety of records at the wrong speeds (faster or slower) and ask everyone to identify the singer and the song. If you want to run this as a competition, then naturally the person who identifies most of the singers and songs correctly is the winner.

481 THAT'S NOT FUNNY, OLD MAN

Adults – Any number – Indoors – Equipment: the judge will need a watch or clock.

Divide the players into two teams, and appoint a judge. The idea is that within a given time limit (say, thirty seconds) the whole of one team must try to make each member in turn of the other team smile or laugh with a joke, a funny face or a tickle. Anyone who does, is out – and the person judged to have kept the straightest face is the winner.

482 THE POLAROID GAME

Icebreaker – For adults – Any number (within reason!) – Indoors – Equipment: a Polaroid Camera.

Take a photograph of the right hand of each arriving guest, and number it (keeping a list of which number belongs to which person). The guests then have to identify the hands.

483 SUPERSTITIONS

Adults – Any number – Indoors – Equipment: pencil and paper for each guest.

Each player is asked to list all the superstitions he or she can think of within five minutes. The player with the longest list wins.

484 GUESS THE GUEST

Adults – Any number – Indoors – Equipment: a tape-recorder.

This game is great fun and well worth a little preparation beforehand. Each guest is asked to make a brief recording on tape (and the more the voice is disguised, the better), the recording is played at the party, and the voice has to be guessed by the other guests. If you can't get hold of your guests before the party takes place, buttonhole them as they arrive, get them to make the recording, and then play it later in the evening.

485 HEADLINES

Adults — Any number — Indoors — Equipment: the front-page head-lines from newspapers of the previous week.

For a week before your party, cut out the front-page headlines from the daily papers (making a note of which one appeared on which day). The guests have to guess which headline appeared on which day of the week — and the most accurate wins. This one's not as simple as it sounds.

486 WHO'S THIS, THEN?

Icebreaker — For adults — Indoors — Equipment: collect in advance of the party if possible a photograph of each guest when a child.

This is a great way to get the party off to a flying start. Collect in advance a photograph of each guest when a child (or, better still, when a baby). The fun starts when the guests have to decide which fellow-guest is shown in which picture.

487 THE CONNOISSEUR

Definitely for adults — Any number — Indoors — Equipment: as wide a variety of drinks as you can muster (and afford), glasses.

Get in as many different bottles of wine as you can, and soak off the labels (remembering to keep a note yourself of what's in which bottle!). Then conduct a 'wine-tasting', where each guest is offered only a sip of each wine and then has to identify it. And if you have any would-be wine snobs in the company, may heaven help you! Try putting the same wine in twice as a hazard.

488 ONE-SYLLABLE CHAT

Teenagers or adults — Any number in pairs — Indoors — Equipment: none.

This one sounds simple, but can be surprisingly difficult. A time limit is set — say, two minutes — and during this period each couple must hold a rational conversation using words of one syllable *only*. The couple who come nearest to talking in this way during the allotted time wins.

489 THE WEIGH-IN

Adults — Any even number — Indoors — Equipment: a pair of bath-room scales, pencil and paper for the judge.

Divide the players into two teams and appoint a judge. Each team member is then taken into another room by the judge, weighed on the scales, and his weight noted. When all the players have been weighed, the judge totals the combined weight for each team.

The object of the game is for each team to assess the weight of each member of the opposing team – and they may do this by lifting them up, prodding them and so on – and then to take a guess at the *combined* weight of the whole team. They are allowed to discuss this amongst themselves before offering a final figure. The team which submits the most accurate final figure for the combined weight of the opposing team wins.

490 THE RICE RACE

Any age over 6 or 7 – Any number – Indoors – Equipment: a pair of kitchen scales, a teaspoon for each player, and some rice.

Each contestant has to run from one end of the room to the other carrying a heaped teaspoonful of rice. There is a 'weigh-in' of the rice before each competitor starts, and another 'weigh-in' when he finishes. The player who's lost the least rice *en route* wins. If there are a large number of players, the game can be adapted into a relay race, with teams transferring rice by teaspoon from a bowl at one end of the room to a bowl at the other – again, the 'weigh-in' applies.

491 RED LETTER

Any age from 9 or 10 – Any number – Indoors – Equipment: pencils and paper.

Each player marks the following headings on a sheet of paper: A Boy's Name, A Girl's Name, A Town Name, A Bird, An Animal, A Tree, A Flower, A Trade. Then the leader chooses a letter of the alphabet at random and everyone has one minute in which to write down a word beginning with that letter under every heading. The player who names the most wins each round.

492 CONGA LINE

Icebreaker – Teenagers – Any number – Indoors – Equipment: radio or record-player.

A Conga line is a party dance, good for getting new arrivals into the party spirit. Each player places his hands on the waist of the person in front. Then the leader dances round the room to the music and all the other players follow his movements.

These are the conga steps. One, two, pause, kick out the right leg. One, two, pause, kick out the left leg . . . and so on.

493 MULTIPLICATION DANCE

Icebreaker — Teenagers — Equal number of boys and girls — Indoors — Equipment: radio or record-player.

A boy and a girl start to dance — any old dance to any sort of music. Whoever is in charge of the radio or record-player stops the music suddenly. Both boy and girl choose a fresh partner and start to dance again. Next time the music stops, the four partners all split up and find themselves new dancing partners. Very soon, everyone in the room is dancing.

494 BALLOON BONANZA

Any age from 6 or 7 — Any number — Indoors — Equipment: 1 balloon, 1 message and 1 present for each child.

This little game requires some advance preparation, but young guests appreciate it. Take some balloons (one for each guest) and before they are blown up, slip inside the neck a message written on a piece of paper. The message tells the whereabouts of a hidden prize. For instance ; 'A bar of chocolate is hidden under the clock', or : 'You will find a present if you look behind the armchair'.

   You have, of course, planted these little surprises in the correct places. The balloons are then blown up and tied at the necks. When the time is right, push all the balloons into the room, tell each child to choose one, burst it — and go to it !

495 GOURMETS

Teenagers or aduıts — Any number — Indoors — Equipment: a varied selection of fruit and vegetables cut into cubes and put on plates, a blindfold.

Cut pieces of raw potato, apple, turnip and so on into cubes, and place on separate plates. Each contestant in turn is blindfolded and fed with the food. He has to guess what he is eating, and the person with the highest score wins. The game can be made harder by putting sugar on the potato, and so on.

496 STREAMER TEARING RACE

Any age from 9 or 10 — 2 teams of equal numbers — Indoors — Equipment: newspaper streamers.

You need some old paper streamers for this game. Cut several exactly the same length — one for every player. Two teams are formed and the leaders start by taking their roll of streamer and very, very carefully tearing along lengthways. When they have finished, Number Twos start tearing theirs. If the streamers are snapped, the team loses a point. The winning team is the first to finish, or the one with the least demerit points.

497 PASS THE CUP RACE

Any age over 7 or 8 — Any even number — Indoors — Equipment: 3 paper cups for each team.

Divide the players into two teams and sit each team in a row. The cups must then be passed along the row with each player using his feet only. The best way to do this is for Number One in the team to hold the cup between his feet, and then slip it on to the toes of player Number Two's outstretched foot. Player Number Three then uses both his feet to take the cup from Number Two and place it on the toes of Number Four's foot — and so on. The players can move about on their chairs, so long as they remain seated. If a cup is dropped, it has to be returned to the end of the line and passed down again. First team to pass all the cups down the line wins. If you want to make the game easier, ask the players to remove their shoes before they begin.

498 BLIND PUFF

Any age from 8 or 9 — Small groups at a time — Indoors — Equipment: 1 large candle.

A large lighted candle is placed in the centre of a table. The players are blindfolded, turned round three times beside the table and then asked to blow out the candle. The first one to do so is the winner. *This game must be supervised by an adult.*

499 CIRCLE HOP

Any age over 5 – Any number – Outdoors – Equipment: chalk to draw circles.

Mark out a row of circles (use small stones for this if you're playing on grass) and line the players up at one end of the row. On the word 'GO' each player must hop on one foot from one circle to the next. If he puts a foot outside the circle, he drops out of the game. The last person left is the winner.

500 MAGNET FISHING

Any age over 5 or 6 – Any even number – Indoors or outdoors – Equipment: 2 sticks or canes, 2 small magnets, string, paper, a bucket or basin, pencil and paper for the score-keeper.

This needs a bit of preparation beforehand. Tie a piece of string with a small magnet on the end on to each of two sticks – these are the fishing rods.

Cut out as many pieces of paper as you fancy in the shape of fish – about six inches long – and write a score mark on each – 1 for a herring, 3 for a haddock, 5 for a salmon and so on. Put a paperclip at the mouth of each fish. The fish are then mixed up and put in a bucket or basin and the teams, taking it in turn to fish, have to see which can catch the highest score. Fish are thrown back after the score is noted and each fisherman has one turn only in competition with his opposite number from the other team.